Daily Gratitude

Publications International, Ltd.

Contributing writer: Joanne Mattern

Cover art: Shutterstock.com

Interior art: Art Explosion, Sharon K. Broutzas, Corbis, Getty, Henry G. Nepomuceno, Shutterstock.com

Louis Weber, CEO
Publications International, Ltd.
8140 Lehigh Avenue
Morton Grove, Illinois 60053

ISBN: 978-1-68022-142-8

Manufactured in China.

8 7 6 5 4 3 2 1

Thanks Be to God

Colossians 2:6–7 says, "As ye have therefore received Christ Jesus the Lord, so walk ye in him: Rooted and built up in him, and stablished in the faith, as ye have been taught, abounding therein with thanksgiving." When we're rooted in prayer, we can't help but notice and be thankful for all the blessings God provides. And as we practice gratitude, we notice more and more to be grateful for!

This book contains a meditation or prayer for each day of the year, focusing on the theme of gratitude, meant to help you reflect on the blessings of your own life. They're offered as a starting place for your communication with God—some can be prayed word by word, while others may act as a springboard for your own prayer, in your own words, tailored for the specifics of your life. They'll help you focus your thoughts and prayers on thanksgiving during the course of a year of God's wonderful blessings.

My List of Blessings

January 1

A land which the Lord thy God careth for: the eyes of the Lord thy God are always upon it, from the beginning of the year even unto the end of the year.

—Deuteronomy 11:12

God of beginnings, be with us as we ring in the New Year! Be with my family and friends, my church, my community, my nation, and this whole wide world of people who are waking up to a fresh start. And please be with me, too! Thank you, Lord, for all you have in store for me this year. Let me be a willing partner in your plans.

January 2

I can feel you calling me, Lord, calling me to make this a year of gratitude and thanksgiving. When I look around at the world and my own life, I want to see the signs of your presence instead of only seeing the negatives. When I pray, I want to do so with a spirit of thanksgiving, not a spirit of complaint.

I've had New Year's resolutions founder in the past, had pledges to go to the gym more often or bicycle to work forgotten by February. Please help me keep this one.

January 3

Offer unto God thanksgiving;
and pay thy vows unto the most High.

—Psalm 50:14

If I need to be reminded of the importance of gratitude, I need only to turn to your Word. Throughout the ages, the Psalms exhort those who read them to give thanks to the Lord. One of the repeated refrains in the Psalms is this simple verse: "O give thanks unto the Lord; for he is good: for his mercy endureth for ever."

Let me not just repeat those words unthinkingly, paying them lip service. Let me say them from the heart.

January 4

The Psalms are a good reminder that when I'm in conversation with you, I don't need to paper over pain with cheery words. Thousands of years later, the emotions of the Psalms ring true, whether the writers are speaking of current trials or of obstacles that have been overcome, praising you or calling on you for help. Let my words to you be honest, Lord. Let my gratitude be honest, not just something I feel I'm "supposed to do."

January 5

I will praise thee with my whole heart:
before the gods will I sing praise unto thee.

I will worship toward thy holy temple, and praise thy
name for thy lovingkindness and for thy truth: for thou
hast magnified thy word above all thy name.

In the day when I cried thou answeredst me, and
strengthenedst me with strength in my soul.

All the kings of the earth shall praise thee, O Lord, when
they hear the words of thy mouth.

Yea, they shall sing in the ways of the Lord:
for great is the glory of the Lord.

—Psalm 138:1–5

January 6

*When they saw the star, they rejoiced
with exceeding great joy.*

—Matthew 2:10

The gospel of Matthew tells the story of the wise men, who searched for Jesus in the days following his birth. As the Christmas season winds down, as we pack away the decorations and put away the ornaments, let me remember to seek you as diligently and wholeheartedly as

the wise men, who set off on a journey when they saw the star. May I be willing to follow you in trust and gratitude when I see the signs of your presence in my life, nudging me to destinations beyond my dreams.

January 7

Sometimes it's the little things, Lord. It's the little things that get to me and cause me stress: the driver who cuts me off in traffic, the spill at dinner, my own foolish mistakes. But it's also the little things that can restore me: a compliment at work, a quick hug from a friend, a favorite hymn being sung at church. Please grant me peace and calm to deal with the little problems of life, and an open heart to notice and appreciate the little joys.

January 8

Thank you for my church community, for the way you led me here, to this place and these people.

My church community isn't free of problems. We have our share of squabbles and friction, like any family does. There are even people I just don't like very much sometimes. When I'm exasperated with someone, please help me to see them through your eyes, and love them with your tenderness. Let me be an instrument of reconciliation and unity, because despite our divisions, we're all here to serve you.

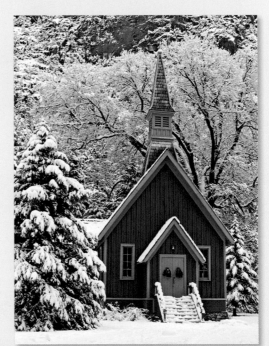

January 9

For thy Church which evermore

Lifteth holy hands above,

Offering up on every shore

Her pure sacrifice of love,

Lord of all, to thee we raise

This our grateful hymn of praise.

Folliot Sandford Pierpoint,
"For the Beauty of the Earth"

January 10

Know ye not that ye are the temple of God, and that the Spirit of God dwelleth in you?

—1 Corinthians 3:16

Creator God, thank you for this body. Thank you for the gift of movement, the gift of touch, the gift of laughter. When I'm at odds with my body, please help me focus my thoughts to what my body can do and the ways it can serve you. Thank you for the nerves and synapses, arteries and brain cells, that make me who I am, your creation.

January 11

Thank you for my family—the closest members who share my daily life and the larger extended family of nieces and nephews, aunts and uncles, cousins and in-laws. I ask you to be with them today, to send your angels to watch over them. I ask you to bring healing to those who are suffering physically or mentally, comfort to those who sorrow, and a clear path to those who are struggling with a decision.

January 12

We're in the bright, cold days of winter now. Thank you for these days and for the brightness of the stars at night. I ask your blessings on the snowplow operators working through the nights of snowfall, the generous people who shovel their neighbors' walkways, and the doctors, nurses, technicians and pharmacists who struggle to work in bad weather.

January 13

I will praise the name of God with a song,
and will magnify him with thanksgiving.

—Psalm 69:30

Thank you for music, in all its wondrous varieties, from the child singing nonsense songs to the community band to the harmony of the great choirs. Music is such a great gift. Let me use my voice to praise you, God!

January 14

And God gave Solomon wisdom and understanding
exceeding much, and largeness of heart,
even as the sand that is on the sea shore.

—1 Kings 4:29

God of wisdom, thank you for all the wise ones who came before, the writers of hymns who spread your word through song the writers of books who shared your wisdom with the world. Thank you for those who share their wisdom and understanding now, who take on the challenge of teaching Sunday school or leading Bible study groups. Pour your blessings upon them, and fill them with your wisdom and understanding.

January 15

He causeth the grass to grow for the cattle,
and herb for the service of man:
that he may bring forth food out of the earth.

—Psalm 104:14

Thank you for the food that nourishes us. Let me remember to thank you before meals, whether I'm

grabbing something on the go, pulling out a bagged lunch at work, or sitting down with my family in the evening. Thank you for the abundant variety of flavors and spices and herbs in the world. Please bless the food I eat today, and the people who grew and harvested the ingredients.

January 16

Meals don't just sustain the body, Lord. When I gather with friends or family over a meal, the community we build nourishes my spirit. Thank you for this great gift, the sharing and laughter that take place over plates of ravioli and rice and potatoes. Please bless the cooks who provide our meals at restaurants, the contributors to our church potlucks, and all those parents and grandparents who are feeding their families tonight. Bless my own cooking and the people with whom I share it.

January 17

Sometimes there are days when everything seems to go wrong, in ways large and small. Sometimes there are days when I seem to do everything wrong—whether it's by making honest mistakes or making choices I knew were wrong.

When I'm anxious, angry, snappish, or out of sorts, please grant me the wisdom to stop and seek you. Help me to forgive the mistakes and wrongs of others. And thank you, always, for your great mercy in forgiving my own wrongs.

January 18

And, behold, two blind men sitting by the way side,
when they heard that Jesus passed by, cried out, saying,
Have mercy on us, O Lord, thou son of David.
And the multitude rebuked them,
because they should hold their peace:
but they cried the more, saying, Have mercy on us,
O Lord, thou son of David. And Jesus stood still,
and called them, and said, What will ye
that I shall do unto you? They say unto him, Lord,
that our eyes may be opened. So Jesus had compassion
on them, and touched their eyes: and immediately
their eyes received sight, and they followed him.

—Matthew 20:30–34

Like those in the Bible who called on you in trust,
I call on you today, Lord. Thank you for your great
compassion.

January 19

Thou wilt shew me the path of life:
in thy presence is fulness of joy;
at thy right hand there are pleasures for evermore.

—Psalm 16:11

O God of joy, thank you for the gift of laughter: the silly laughter of a young child who is just learning to tell jokes, the contagious laughter at the dinner table, or the appreciative laughter when grandpa tells a family story.

January 20

Thank you for the things that could have gone wrong but didn't—the close calls, the accidents that were averted, the diagnosis of something minor when the symptoms pointed to something more serious. In that moment when my muscles loosen and I give a deep sigh of relief, let me remember to thank you, my saving God.

January 21

Thank you for all the things that provide warmth in cold places, Lord! Thank you for thermoses of hot chocolate, carefully made quilts passed down in the family, and brightly-colored scarves.

In these winter days, I pray for those who don't have shelter and warmth. Give me a spirit of generosity and discernment in order to best help those in need of coats, blankets, or aid with their electricity bills.

January 22

And whatsoever ye do, do it heartily, as to the Lord,
and not unto men.

—Colossians 3:23

Thank you for work, Lord. Whether it's making a home, volunteering, or working for pay, let me do the work you've called me to at this point in my life with attention and care. Be with me as I go about my daily tasks.

January 23

Thank you for the children! Childhood is such a remarkable time, and seeing the children in my life learn and grow and change is such a delight. Please give me patience and an inquiring spirit in response to their curiosity, gentleness and a listening ear to soothe their hurts, and wisdom and a loving heart to set them on the right path when they err.

January 24

If thou draw out thy soul to the hungry,
and satisfy the afflicted soul;
then shall thy light rise in obscurity,
and thy darkness be as the noon day.

—Isaiah 58:10

Thank you for unexpected kindness. Sometimes
in times of crisis or loss, my closest friends
and family have been busy dealing with their
own problems or grief. But other people have
stepped in: a colleague who covered my work, an
acquaintance from church who brought by food,
or a neighbor who volunteered childcare. Thank
you, Lord, for those who have reached out to me
when I have been the one in need. Please grant
me the grace to be generous in turn.

January 25

Now there are diversities of gifts, but the same Spirit.
—1 Corinthians 12:4

God, thank you for the talents and gifts you give each of us to serve your church. Let me not be envious of the gifts of others or proud of my own. Let me serve you with a humble heart.

January 26

*Blessed be the Lord, who daily loadeth us with benefits,
even the God of our salvation.*

—Psalm 68:19

Thank you, Lord,
for the everyday.
Thank you for the
patterns that make
up my life: the daily
routine, the weekly
call to worship
together, the change
of the seasons, and
the yearly holidays. I
will bless your name
all the days of my life.

January 27

Thank you for newness and change, God! Thank you for the spark of a new idea and the changes to routine brought by new additions to my family and my group of friends. Let me never be so bound by tradition that I fail to recognize your hand at work, setting me gently on a new path.

January 28

And he said, Come. And when Peter was come down out
of the ship, he walked on the water, to go to Jesus.
But when he saw the wind boisterous, he was afraid;
and beginning to sink, he cried, saying, Lord, save me.
And immediately Jesus stretched forth his hand,
and caught him, and said unto him,
O thou of little faith, wherefore didst thou doubt?
—Matthew 14:29–31

Sometimes I falter
in my faith. Even
during those times,
Jesus, you are with
me as you were with
Peter. Thank you for
always catching me.

January 29

A new heart also will I give you,
and a new spirit will I put within you:
and I will take away the stony heart out of your flesh,
and I will give you an heart of flesh.

—Ezekiel 36:26

Even if I fail you, Lord, you never fail me.
Thank you for your mercy and forgiveness.
Let me respond to them with a grateful heart.

January 30

Whoso trusteth in the Lord, happy is he.

—Proverbs 16:20

I thank you for the good days, God! I'm grateful for the days when things go smoothly, the days that are free of anxiety and care. Thank you for the presentation at work that went over well, the travel time that was shorter than anticipated, and the good grades brought home by the children. Thank you for today's successes!

January 31

The days are getting longer, Lord! Thank you, Light of the World, for this reminder that winter will recede and spring return.

As January closes, thank you for all that's gone well during this past month. For those times when I was imperfect, when I strayed from you, I ask for forgiveness. Thank you always for your comforting presence and your steadfast, overflowing love.

February 1

A new commandment I give unto you,
That ye love one another; as I have loved you,
that ye also love one another.
By this shall all men know that ye are my disciples,
if ye have love one to another.

—John 13:34–35

February can be a difficult month. The dregs of winter are here: gray skies, slush, and potholes. But February is also a month in which we remember love—not just romantic love, but all love, which ultimately proceeds from you. This month, let me be grateful for those who have loved me and their presence in my life. Let me be loving towards all those you have brought into my life.

February 2

For the joy of human love,

Brother, sister, parent, child,

Friends on earth, and friends above;

For all gentle thoughts and mild:

Christ, our God, to Thee we raise

This our Sacrifice of Praise.

Folliot Sandford Pierpoint,
"For the Beauty of the Earth"

February 3

The father of the righteous shall greatly rejoice:
and he that begetteth a wise child shall have joy of him.
Thy father and thy mother shall be glad,
and she that bare thee shall rejoice.

—Proverbs 23:24–25

Thank you, God, for my childhood family. Bless the parents who loved me and raised me. I'm grateful for the financial sacrifices they made and for the time and care they took. Grant me a forgiving heart for their shortcomings and imperfections. Keep our relationship strong, even as it changes over time.

They protected me as a child. I ask you to keep them safe always, to hold them in your loving arms. Help them keep growing in your love and wisdom.

February 4

Thank you for my sisters and brothers and cousins, and for those friends who have become over time brothers and sisters of the heart. We've shared so much over the years! Please continue to bless our times together.

I ask you to shower blessings upon them: safety, health, meaningful work, and the gift of loving people in their lives.

February 5

The counsel of the Lord standeth for ever,
the thoughts of his heart to all generations.

—Psalm 33:11

Thank you for the members of my extended family: those from the generations before, who shared their stories and wisdom; those from my generation, with whom I share so much history; and those who are just growing up now. I'm closer to some than to others (and I admit to finding some of them downright difficult), but they all bring something to the family, and they're loved by people important to me. Send your angels to guard them and keep watch over them.

February 6

Many waters cannot quench love,
neither can the floods drown it.

—Song of Solomon 8:7

Thank you for romantic love, Lord, for
the deep and abiding love between spouses.
Bless the couples I know, the families
they've built together, and the traditions
they've created.

Thank you for the one I love, Lord.
Thank you for the events that brought us
together and the love that binds us now.
Keep us talking to each other and relying
on each other, so that we grow together
and do not grow apart. Above all, keep us
growing together in our love for you.

February 7

*L*ord, thank you for my children, by birth or of the heart—all the children for whom I've taken on the role of parent or stepparent or grandparent or loving aunt.

*F*ather God, sending children out into the world can be scary. Please don't let my fears or worries keep them from the path you intend for them to follow. Let me be loving in words and actions, so that even when I'm angry with them, they never doubt my love. Give me the right words at the right times to teach them your ways.

February 8

Ruth said, Intreat me not to leave thee,
or to return from following after thee.

—Ruth 1:16

Thank you for those people who have
become part of our family through
relationships, engagements, and marriages.
Let us be welcoming, Lord, never so tied
up in family traditions that we inadvertently
exclude a new in-law. Instead, let us be
grateful for new perspectives, new stories to
share, and new connections.

In those situations where I am the new
one, please give us hearts that are open to
each other. Let us be like Naomi and Ruth,
building a strong and lasting connection.

February 9

A friend loveth at all times.

—Proverbs 17:17

Thank you for my friends. Thank you for bringing these wonderful people into my life. Looking back, I can't always trace the progress from first meeting to acquaintanceship to friendship, but I know I'm grateful that we built the friendship we did.

Let me be a good friend, generous with my time and love.

February 10

As cold waters to a thirsty soul,
so is good news from a far country.

—Proverbs 25:25

Thank you for friends in faraway places. In some cases we've drifted apart with distance, but when I see them during vacations or get an e-mail from them, it seems as if we spoke only yesterday. Bless their spouses and children, their endeavors and their work.

February 11

The heart of the wise teacheth his mouth,
and addeth learning to his lips.

—Proverbs 16:23

Thank you for those who have taught me, Lord. Bless those who have shared their knowledge with me, whether in the classroom, at the workplace, or at my church. Bless those who have led me and many others closer to you.

February 12

Thank you for those who work to heal the body and mind. Doctors, nurses, therapists, medical technicians, pharmacists—all the people to whom we turn for answers and aid. Thank you for those who have been kind and patient with their explanations, who have gone above and beyond the call of duty.

Help them, healing God. Help them with the stressful situations they must deal with. Guide their eyes and their minds and their hands as they diagnose problems and ease pain.

February 13

Thank you for those I see in the course of daily life, like cashiers, waitstaff, security guards, and taxi drivers. Thank you for those who do their jobs well—let me not take that for granted and forget to express my appreciation. Help me be patient when our interactions are going badly, and to point out any errors gently, always remembering that they're your children as much as I am. And even if I'm justly angry at the policies of a company, even as I stand firm for what's right, let me not take it out on the representatives of that company.

February 14

And we have known and believed the love that
God hath to us. God is love; and he that dwelleth
in love dwelleth in God, and God in him.

—1 John 4:16

Loving God, how can
I express my gratitude
for your love? You, who
have seen all my faults
and fears, love me—
without limitations,
with overflowing
abundance. Abba,
Father, I thank you and
praise your holy name.

February 15

Thank you for the leaders, Lord. At church, at work, in my local and regional communities, at the national level—bless those who use their talents for leadership on our behalf. Grant them your wisdom, the gift of discernment, and courage to follow always the path of righteousness.

Where I disagree with those in office, please grant me courage to speak up against their actions. But please also help me not to react out of knee-jerk anger, and not to forget that they, too, are loved by you.

February 16

Beloved, if God so loved us,
we ought also to love one another.

—1 John 4:11

O God, you know and I know that not all my relationships are rooted in love. Some relationships have been broken and fractured by my actions or those of the other person.

It's hard, Lord, to remember a closeness that no longer exists. Let me not flinch away from the brokenness, but bring it to you. Only then will I  find peace. Thank you for your healing and your comfort.

February 17

For I know that my redeemer liveth,
and that he shall stand at the latter day upon the earth.

—Job 19:25

Today I remember those loved ones who have passed from this earth. Lord, thank you for their presence in my life. Thank you for the time we shared. It makes me smile just to think of them. How much I treasured their friendship and their love! They truly lived out your message of love, Lord.

February 18

And seeing the multitudes, he went up into a mountain:
and when he was set, his disciples came unto him:
And he opened his mouth, and taught them, saying,
Blessed are the poor in spirit:
for theirs is the kingdom of heaven.

—Matthew 5:1–3

Lord, thank you for
your teachings. Deepen
my understanding of the
familiar words and let them
guide my decisions and
actions. I want to seek your
kingdom with a humble and
contrite heart. I don't want
to be distracted by desire for
the possessions of this world.
I want to yearn for you.

February 19

Blessed are they that mourn: for they shall be comforted.

—Matthew 5:4

Thank you for the promise of comfort in times of mourning. Being your child does not mean that we will never suffer, that we will never have to deal with loss. But we know that you will be there in the midst of suffering.

February 20

Blessed are the meek:
for they shall inherit the earth.

—Matthew 5:5

"Meek" isn't a word we hear that often nowadays. Meekness certainly isn't encouraged by our society. But in the Bible, meekness, gentleness, humility, lowliness—all these are valued. Numbers 12:3 describes Moses as "very meek," and in Matthew 11:29, Jesus describes himself as "meek and lowly in heart." The Psalms and the prophet Isaiah promise rewards to the meek (cf. Psalm 22:26 and Isaiah 61:1), and Paul encourages the virtue (Galatians 6:1, Colossians 3:12). Lord, teach me to value meekness. Thank you for those people in my life who are shining examples of gentleness and humility and who model the virtue for me.

February 21

*Blessed are they which do hunger
and thirst after righteousness:
for they shall be filled.*

—Matthew 5:6

Thank you for those who
seek righteousness, for
those who want to see a just
world, and for those who
want nothing more than to
act in accordance with your
will. Thank you for those
who speak for the voiceless
and disadvantaged, spending
their time, money, and
talent in fighting against
oppression and injustice.

February 22

Blessed are the merciful: for they shall obtain mercy.

—Matthew 5:7

Merciful God, thank you for your mercy and forgiveness. Thank you for those who have shown mercy to me when I needed it. Thank you for those times when you have worked through me to extend mercy and forgiveness to those who needed it.

February 23

Blessed are the pure in heart: for they shall see God.

—Matthew 5:8

What a promise, Lord—to see you and bask in your glory. Every so often, I've encountered someone who seems to be illuminated from within, who just shines spiritually with the simplicity and clarity of the truly pure at heart. Thank you for putting those people in my path. Please give me purity of heart, Lord. Let me be as the writer of Psalm 42, knowing that, "As the hart panteth after the water brooks, so panteth my soul after thee, O God."

February 24

Blessed are the peacemakers:
for they shall be called the children of God.

—Matthew 5:9

Prince of Peace,
thank you for those who
follow in your ways in
seeking peace. Thank
you for those times
when your Spirit has
been at work in me, so
that I chose peace over
anger and resentment.
Let your peace flourish
in my home, my church
and my nation!

February 25

Blessed are they which are persecuted
for righteousness' sake:
for theirs is the kingdom of heaven.
Blessed are ye, when men shall revile you,
and persecute you, and shall say all manner
of evil against you falsely, for my sake.
Rejoice, and be exceeding glad:
for great is your reward in heaven:
for so persecuted they the prophets
which were before you.

—Matthew 5:10–12

This isn't an easy verse to read! I don't want to think about encountering persecution. I don't want to think about those I love suffering either. Sometimes I'd rather stay in a safe cocoon and not make waves. Please help me be grateful instead of afraid when the opportunity comes to speak up for your truth.

February 26

*Be careful for nothing; but in every thing by prayer
and supplication with thanksgiving
let your requests be made known unto God.*

—Philippians 4:6

*L*et me always remember that all the gifts I receive, all I
am, comes from you. I can turn my worries over to you,
knowing that you will answer my needs. Thank you, God.

February 27

I thank thee, and praise thee,
O thou God of my fathers,
who hast given me wisdom and might,
and hast made known unto me now
what we desired of thee:
for thou hast now made known unto us
the king's matter.

—Daniel 2:23

Lord, sometimes
someone comes to me
with worries or concerns,
and I find words pouring
out, words of wisdom
that I know come from
you. Thank you for using
me as your instrument to
help others.

February 28

O Lord my God,
I will give thanks unto thee for ever.

—Psalm 30:12

For this day,

For the sun and the moon,

For the food we eat,

For the conversation we share,

For the blessings you give,

I thank you, Lord most high.

February 29

Now thank we all our God,
with heart and hands and voices,

Who wondrous things has done,
in Whom this world rejoices;

Who from our mothers' arms
has blessed us on our way

With countless gifts of love,
and still is ours today.

Martin Rinkart, trans.
Catherine Winkworth,
"Now Thank We All Our God"

March 1

O Lord, how manifold are thy works!
in wisdom hast thou made them all:
the earth is full of thy riches.

—Psalm 104:24

Thank you for curiosity
and the gift of discovering
something new. There's so
much wonder in this world
when I take the time to read
and explore. Rocks and
minerals, strange undersea
animals, the far reaches of
space…sometimes when
I learn about something
you've created, I just have
to say, "Wow!"

March 2

And he hath filled him with the spirit of God,
in wisdom, in understanding, and in knowledge,
and in all manner of workmanship;
And to devise curious works, to work in gold,
and in silver, and in brass, And in the cutting of stones,
to set them, and in carving of wood,
to make any manner of cunning work.
—Exodus 35:31–33

Thank you for the gift of human intelligence and ingenuity. Quilt patterns and crocheted shawls, microscopes and paintings, rockets and automobiles—thank you for the inspiration to create beautiful and useful things. Let us always remember that ultimately our gifts come from you.

March 3

*Let no corrupt communication proceed out of
your mouth, but that which is good to the use of edifying,
that it may minister grace unto the hearers.*

—Ephesians 4:29

Thank you for the
gift of communication.
We live in an age where
we can send messages
to loved ones across
continents in the blink
of an eye—how amazing!
In this age of abundant
communication, help
me to keep my words
and speech fruitful,
kind, and truthful.

March 4

*Beloved, I wish above all things that thou mayest prosper
and be in health, even as thy soul prospereth.*

—3 John 1:2

Thank you for your gift of healing and recovery. When
I can feel my body begin to mend and my energy begin to
return after an illness, I am filled with immense gratitude.

In times of illness,
let me turn to you.
In times of health,
let me never forget
that health is a gift I
owe to you.

March 5

Give thanks for the ordinary

and the extraordinary,

the work week and the Sabbath day,

the days of feast and our daily bread.

Give thanks for gray mornings

and spectacular sunsets,

rainy days and meteor showers,

cloth of cotton and jewelry of gold.

Give thanks for the trees

in all their seasons,

the desert sand and the cactus in bloom,

the still pond and the rushing river,

flowing over with life.

March 6

I will have mercy, and not sacrifice:
for I am not come to call the righteous,
but sinners to repentance.

—Matthew 9:13

In the days that lead up to Easter, let me truly examine my life and turn it over to you, Lord. Let me be ever grateful for Jesus' sacrifice on the cross.

March 7

Come now, and let us reason together,
saith the Lord: though your sins be as scarlet,
they shall be as white as snow;
though they be red like crimson, they shall be as wool.

—Isaiah 1:18

Sometimes I'm afraid to look too closely at my faults and failings. It's as if I'm a small child, closing my eyes in the hopes that if I can't see them, you won't see them. But you do see them, and when I acknowledge and repent of them, you wash them clean. Thank you for your enduring mercy, God of forgiveness.

March 8

When thou gatherest the grapes of thy vineyard,
thou shalt not glean it afterward:
it shall be for the stranger, for the fatherless,
and for the widow.

—Deuteronomy 24:21

Thank you for the basics of life: food, shelter, and clothing. I sometimes take them for granted until they're threatened by unemployment or natural disaster. Help me to remember my gratitude in times of bounty, and to share these blessings with those who might be going through times of scarcity.

March 9

And when she was risen up to glean,
Boaz commanded his young men,
saying, Let her glean even among the sheaves,
and reproach her not: And let fall also some
of the handfuls of purpose for her, and leave them,
that she may glean them, and rebuke her not.

—Ruth 2:15–16

I am so grateful, Lord, for the kindness of those who have been generous during lean times: the friend who took me out to lunch when I was living paycheck-to-paycheck, the person from church who dropped off a batch of hand-me-downs for the children, and the aunt who dropped by with groceries. We're encouraged to be self-sufficient, and it can be a blow to the pride to accept charity. Please help me be gracious in accepting the generosity of others, remembering that we are all your children, charged with helping one another.

March 10

Give, and it shall be given unto you;
good measure, pressed down, and shaken together,
and running over, shall men give into your bosom.
For with the same measure that ye mete withal
it shall be measured to you again.

—Luke 6:38

Thank you for volunteers. Thank you for the ones who spend their time and energy in soup kitchens, hospitals, and nursing homes. Bless the lawyers who take pro bono cases, the accountants who help the elderly with their taxes, and the volunteer docents at museums and parks who happily share their knowledge. May they be blessed tenfold!

March 11

It is more blessed to give than to receive.

—Acts 20:35

𝒯hank you for all that I receive through volunteer work. The work can be challenging, but it is rewarding to serve you by serving others.

March 12

Sing unto the Lord with thanksgiving;
sing praise upon the harp unto our God.

—Psalm 147:7

Thank you for
those who lead us
in music during
worship, serving
as cantors, choir
members, organists,
and handbell ringers.
There is so much joy
in raising our voices
to you in song!

March 13

For the joy of ear and eye,

For the heart and brain's delight,

For the mystic harmony

Linking sense to sound and sight:

Christ, our God, to Thee we raise

This our Sacrifice of Praise.

Folliot Sandford Pierpoint,
"For the Beauty of the Earth"

March 14

If ye walk in my statutes, and keep my commandments,
and do them; Then I will give you rain in due season,
and the land shall yield her increase,
and the trees of the field shall yield their fruit.
—Leviticus 26:3–4

Thank you for rain, God of the heavens! I'm not always grateful for it unless there's been a lack of it. On the days when I see clouds and get grumpy, let me remember that rain is a necessary and blessed gift.

March 15

Let the words of my mouth,
and the meditation of my heart,
be acceptable in thy sight,
O Lord, my strength, and my redeemer.

—Psalm 19:14

Thank you for calling
me to prayer. When I
answer that call daily,
I see how things in my
life run more smoothly.
When I take the time to
sit in silence with you, I
feel your peace pervade
my life.

March 16

Thank you for the stories of the Bible. When I read about the people of the Bible, I am by turns inspired, encouraged, and challenged. When I sit and reflect on your Word, and on how people responded to it in the past, my own relationship with you deepens and grows.

March 17

Thank you for the stories of the patriarchs and matriarchs. They weren't perfect people. Sarah was skeptical; Jacob was a schemer; Rachel and Leah were jealous of each other; the sibling rivalry between Joseph and his brothers nearly ended in tragedy. From their example I learn I don't need to be perfect to be in communication with you.

March 18

Thank you for the example of the leaders: Moses and Joshua, Deborah and Gideon, David and Josiah. The judges and kings didn't always have an easy time of it. Sometimes they doubted, and sometimes they failed you. But they held steadfast to their faith in you. Make me more like Josiah, who set a shining example for his people in doing "that which was right in the sight of the Lord."

March 19

What doth the Lord require of thee,
but to do justly, and to love mercy,
and to walk humbly with thy God?

—Micah 6:8

Thank you for those you send
as prophets. Thank you for the
Biblical prophets, whose words of
repentance and renewal still ring
true today. Thank you also for
those who have played a prophetic
role in my life, who have called
upon me to act justly or change a
sinful behavior. I haven't always
responded well at the time, but
when I look back, I know it wasn't
easy for them to confront me, either.

March 20

*M*any of your prophets were hesitant, even afraid, when they were called or at times during their ministry. Jeremiah thought he was too young. Jonah fled. Elijah at one point despaired and said, "It is enough; now, O Lord, take away my life; for I am not better than my fathers." (1 Kings 19:4) In response, God sent him an angel with food to restore him. During those times when I find it difficult to answer your call, Lord, please help me remember that you will send me what I need to fulfill your mission. Thank you.

March 21

Thank you for the psalmists and for those who collected the wisdom of the ages in Proverbs and Ecclesiastes. Turning to these ancient parts of the Bible, I unexpectedly find verses that apply to my own life and current times. What a gift, God of Ages!

March 22

And Mary said, Behold the handmaid of the Lord;
be it unto me according to thy word.

—Luke 1:38

Thank you for Mary. In her response to the angel,
she accepted great change and even hardship in her
life. What an amazing example of faith to follow!

March 23

Then Joseph being raised from sleep did as the angel
of the Lord had bidden him, and took unto him his wife.

—Matthew 1:24

Thank you for the example of Joseph. He provides
an example of quiet obedience, protection, and
caretaking for others. May I be obedient like Joseph
when I feel you guiding me.

March 24

For God so loved the world, that he gave
his only begotten Son, that whosoever believeth in him
should not perish, but have everlasting life.
For God sent not his Son into the world to condemn
the world; but that the world through him
might be saved.

—John 3:16–17

Thank you for your Son. Jesus, thank you for your ministry, for coming among us to heal and teach. Thank you for saving us through your sacrifice.

How can I thank you enough?

March 25

Thank you for all the stories of people who responded to Jesus: John who leapt in Elizabeth's womb; Anna the prophetess and Simeon the devout man; the disciples who left their boats; the centurion believing that Jesus would heal his servant. Let reading about their faith and their wholehearted response to your Son strengthen my own faith.

March 26

Thank you for the example of Joseph of Arimathea, who took on the responsibility of burying Jesus despite his fear. Thank you for the example of the women who followed Jesus, who mourned him and went with spices and ointments to the tomb. They found it empty. Give me a heart of service like theirs— even when I am scared, even when it seems hopeless.

March 27

Thank you for the leaders of the early Church. What wondrous things you did through them!

Sometimes the stories I've heard from childhood, like the story of Paul's conversion, can feel stale. Breathe fresh life into it when I need to hear it anew, when I need to be surprised by your Spirit.

March 28

And as he entered into a certain village, there met him
ten men that were lepers, which stood afar off:
And they lifted up their voices, and said,
Jesus, Master, have mercy on us.

And when he saw them, he said unto them,
Go shew yourselves unto the priests. And it came to pass,
that, as they went, they were cleansed. And one of them,
when he saw that he was healed, turned back, and with a
loud voice glorified God, And fell down on his face at his
feet, giving him thanks: and he was a Samaritan.

And Jesus answering said, Were there not ten cleansed?
but where are the nine? There are not found
that returned to give glory to God, save this stranger.
And he said unto him, Arise, go thy way:
thy faith hath made thee whole.

—Luke 17:12–19

Lord, let me always remember to thank you!

March 29

And after six days Jesus taketh Peter, James,
and John his brother, and bringeth them up into
an high mountain apart, And was transfigured
before them: and his face did shine as the sun,
and his raiment was white as the light.

—Matthew 17:1–2

Lord, you know that
sometimes I struggle with
faith. I don't feel your
presence. But then there
are moments when I
feel like I'm on the high
mountain, filled with
wonder. Let me be grateful
for those astonishing
moments, and let them
sustain me in desert times.

March 30

We see Peter falter fairly often. He doesn't always understand the words of Jesus. He denies Jesus and regrets it bitterly. But he also proclaims him. He calls Jesus the Messiah, the Son of the Living God.

Jesus, when I fail you, when I skirt away from proclaiming my faith, remind me of Peter's boldness.

March 31

I offer in his tabernacle sacrifices of joy;
I will sing, yea, I will sing praises unto the Lord.

—Psalm 27:6

*L*ooking back over this past month, I can see your hand at work. I offer you praise and thanksgiving for what you have done. I know you will keep working in my life!

April 1

For the preaching of the cross is to them
that perish foolishness; but unto us which are saved
it is the power of God.

—1 Corinthians 1:18

On this day of pranks and silliness, let me remember Paul's words on foolishness and how what is perceived as foolishness by the world is in fact incredible. We are saved and redeemed by your death and resurrection, Lord! Thank you!

April 2

The sights and sounds of renewal and new life are springing up around us! Thank you for this season of rebirth, Lord, for the trees budding and the birds returning. Your creation is full of wonders, and in the season of spring they're easy to spot!

April 3

The heavens declare the glory of God;

and the firmament sheweth his handywork.

Day unto day uttereth speech,

and night unto night sheweth knowledge.

There is no speech nor language,

where their voice is not heard.

Their line is gone out through all the earth,

and their words to the end of the world.

—Psalm 19:1–4

April 4

And God said, Let there be light: and there was light.
And God saw the light, that it was good:
and God divided the light from the darkness.
And God called the light Day,
and the darkness he called Night.
And the evening and the morning were the first day.
—Genesis 1:3–5

Thank you for night and day, for sunrise and sunset. Thank you for the darkness that means it's time to tuck the kids in bed, safe and sound, and the light that means it's time for a new day!

April 5

*And God said, Let there be a firmament in the midst
of the waters, and let it divide the waters
from the waters. And God made the firmament,
and divided the waters which were under the firmament
from the waters which were above the firmament:
and it was so. And God called the firmament Heaven.
And the evening and the morning were the second day.*

—Genesis 1:6-8

Sometimes I wonder what it was
like for you to create the universe.
How did you decide what you
wanted to do? How did you decide
what came next? Were you delighted
by your growing creation?

Praise you, creative God!

April 6

And God said, Let the earth bring forth grass,
the herb yielding seed, and the fruit tree yielding fruit
after his kind, whose seed is in itself, upon the earth:
and it was so. And the earth brought forth grass,
and herb yielding seed after his kind,
and the tree yielding fruit, whose seed was in itself,
after his kind: and God saw that it was good.
And the evening and the morning were the third day.
　　　　　　　　　　　　　　　　—Genesis 1:11–13

Today I thank you for
plants! Food to sustain us,
herbs to season that food,
plants with medicinal
components, flowers to
cheer our spirits—thank
you for all of them!

April 7

And God made two great lights; the greater light
to rule the day, and the lesser light to rule the night:
he made the stars also. And God set them in the
firmament of the heaven to give light upon the earth,
And to rule over the day and over the night,
and to divide the light from the darkness:
and God saw that it was good.
And the evening and the morning were the fourth day.
—Genesis 1:16–19

In cities and towns, the stars can be obscured. We think we're seeing them, but it's not until we go out in the country and look up that we truly see the full glory of a starry night spread above us. Thank you for their beauty, and for those special times when we can see them clearly.

April 8

*And God said, Let the waters bring forth abundantly
the moving creature that hath life, and fowl that may fly
above the earth in the open firmament of heaven.*

—Genesis 1:20

Spring is an active time for birds. It's lovely to hear
them chirping, to point out nests to the kids while we're
on a walk, and to spot different varieties on a hike.
Thank you, God, for the great variety of life around us!

April 9

*And God said, Let the earth bring forth the living
creature after his kind, cattle, and creeping thing,
and beast of the earth after his kind: and it was so.*

—Genesis 1:24

Thank you for the animals that are part of our lives,
especially our pets, who bring such comfort and joy and
playfulness to our lives.

We know more nowadays about how dogs and other

animals can help
people as companion
and therapy animals.
Thank you for them,
Lord, and please bless
the people who train
them and use them.

April 10

So God created man in his own image,
in the image of God created he him;
male and female created he them.

—Genesis 1:27

Thank you for creating us, Lord. What an indescribable gift, to know that we are created in your image. When I interact with my fellow humans, and when I look in the mirror at myself, let me see and remember how you have formed us in your image.

April 11

*And on the seventh day God ended his work
which he had made; and he rested on the seventh day
from all his work which he had made.*

—Genesis 2:2

Thank you for rest, for the gift of satisfied exhaustion after a job well done. Thank you for setting aside time for us to honor you and to remember what you have made. Our society doesn't encourage us to keep the Sabbath Day holy—please help our family remember to do so.

April 12

For the beauty of the earth,

For the beauty of the skies,

For the Love which from our birth

Over and around us lies:

Christ, our God, to Thee we raise

This our Sacrifice of Praise.

Folliot Sandford Pierpoint,
"For the Beauty of the Earth"

April 13

Be still, and know that I am God.

—Psalm 46:10

Thank you for the gift of quiet: a hushed moment of silence in church, an expectant moment of silence while we wait for news, a peaceful moment when no words need to be said. In the Garden, Jesus asked that the disciples watch with him for just one hour. Give me the wisdom, Lord, to know when it is time to sit with you in silence.

April 14

So Solomon built the house, and finished it.

—1 Kings 6:14

Thank you for those who plan our church liturgies, and those who give a gift of their time in singing, reading aloud, or decorating the church. Thank you for those who do work behind the scenes in keeping records, tracking accounts, and cleaning our worship space.

April 15

Thou hast made known to me the ways of life;
thou shalt make me full of joy with thy countenance.

—Acts 2:28

Thank you for your gifts of laughter and joy. When I allow you fully into my life, you bring not just happiness but abundant joy. Thank you, Lord! Let me be your instrument to share that joy with others.

April 16

Thank you for new friendships. Sometimes we meet someone and there's that little pull towards each other, where we enjoy each other's company and find out we have unexpected things in common. It's a delight! When I'm lonely, let me trust that you'll put the people you want me to meet in my pathway.

April 17

Thank you for

relief after pain,

rain after drought,

water after thirst,

healing after illness,

reconciliation after strife,

joy after sorrow.

April 18

Leave there thy gift before the altar, and go thy way;
first be reconciled to thy brother,
and then come and offer thy gift.

—Matthew 5:24

Thank you for restored relationships, Lord. Thank you for those times when a friend or family member has reached out to me to resolve a rift or close a growing distance. You know how much those relationships mean to me, and how good it feels to be at peace again.

There may be times when a relationship can't be repaired—or at least not right now. But please let me be vulnerable enough to reach out and try when I feel you calling me to do so.

April 19

For I am not ashamed of the gospel of Christ:
for it is the power of God unto salvation to every one
that believeth; to the Jew first, and also to the Greek.
—Romans 1:16

God, thank you for those who share your good news, for those in the early church and for those people in my life who shared it with me. It's amazing to think of this chain of believers lasting thousands of years, bound by your love.

Thank you, most of all, for the gift of salvation.

April 20

Thank you for traditions—family traditions, regional traditions, faith traditions. The traditions we share, the way we celebrate certain occasions and the special foods we make and eat, are a source of unity and good memories.

At the same time, let me never value tradition so much that I neglect the needs of the people in my life in order to serve tradition. Let us be guided by love in shaping new traditions when we need to!

April 21

Praise ye the Lord.

Praise God in his sanctuary:

praise him in the firmament of his power.

Praise him for his mighty acts:

praise him according to his excellent greatness.

Praise him with the sound of the trumpet:

praise him with the psaltery and harp.

Praise him with the timbrel and dance:

praise him with stringed instruments and organs.

Praise him upon the loud cymbals:

praise him upon the high sounding cymbals.

Let every thing that hath breath praise the Lord.

Praise ye the Lord.

—Psalm 150

April 22

I will both lay me down in peace, and sleep:
for thou, Lord, only makest me dwell in safety.

—Psalm 4:8

Thank you for the gift of restful sleep. On the nights when I struggle with going to sleep, let your peace fill me and soothe me. Let me turn my cares over to you.

April 23

Every one that thirsteth, come ye to the waters,
and he that hath no money; come ye, buy, and eat;
yea, come, buy wine and milk
without money and without price.

—Isaiah 55:1

This verse is such a comforting one. You meet our needs, the needs of our body and the yearnings of our heart. We don't need to be wealthy or wise or distinguished for you to care about us. When we come to you in humility, you bless us with abundant love.

April 24

But Simon's wife's mother lay sick of a fever,
and anon they tell him of her.
And he came and took her by the hand, and lifted her up;
and immediately the fever left her,
and she ministered unto them.

—Mark 1:30–31

When I have a cold or am suffering through seasonal allergies, I don't feel very grateful for my body. But even when it's working imperfectly, this body is a gift from you. Let me remember to say thank you—even if I'm saying it between sneezes! And when I recover, let me be like Simon Peter's mother-in-law, getting up from illness to return to serving you.

April 25

I disagreed with someone close to me today, and we ended up having a good discussion about the matter. Thank you for being with us today even as we argued— we were willing to listen to each other instead of being hotheaded, and I know that was your blessing.

April 26

Oh, Lord, it hurts when someone I love is struggling through something difficult, like bullying at school, unemployment, or depression. I wish I could shield those I love from harm or swoop in and fix their problems.

When someone does confide their suffering to me, please grant me words of comfort and wisdom. Thank you, healing God, for I know we can always turn to you for solace.

April 27

*And even to your old age I am he; and even to hoar hairs
will I carry you: I have made, and I will bear;
even I will carry, and will deliver you.*

—Isaiah 46:4

Thank you for the wisdom that comes with age
and experience. When I was young, I thought
adults knew everything.
Now that I am one, I
know how much we
don't know! But even
if I'm still muddling
through life in some
ways, I know that my
relationship with you has
grown deeper and richer
over time.

April 28

Who can find a virtuous woman?
for her price is far above rubies.
The heart of her husband doth safely trust in her,
so that he shall have no need of spoil.

—Proverbs 31:10-11

Thank you for time spent with my spouse— thank you for bringing us together, to build a family and to take care of each other. Let me not take the work that my spouse does for granted. Let me be good to my spouse as we jointly take care of our family.

April 29

He appointed the moon for seasons:
the sun knoweth his going down.

—Psalm 104:19

As spring progresses, certain foods are coming back into season. It's time to pull out certain recipes from the cookbook: salmon, asparagus, peas, and salads. Thank you for the cycle of the seasons that makes familiar things fresh again!

April 30

Thank you for the family stories and memories that have been passed down. As I grow older, I find myself thinking more about those from past generations who died when I was young. Through stories, I feel connected to them. Thank you for those of the next generation, who are adding to the store of family stories!

May 1

Honour thy father and thy mother: that thy days may be
long upon the land which the Lord thy God giveth thee.

—Exodus 20:12

In this month of Mother's Day, I thank you for mothers! Grant peace to new mothers who are worrying or short on sleep, strength to mothers whose children are ill or being bullied, guidance to stepmothers who are blending families together, and wisdom to foster mothers and adoptive mothers and the children they welcome into their homes.

Thank you for my mother, so close to my heart. Grant her your blessing today and draw her closer to you always.

May 2

May is Mental Health Awareness Month in the U.S. In this month, I thank you for being present to those who suffer from mental illness. Help them feel your presence and know the peace that comes with your love. Please be with the members of their support system: family, friends, therapists, and caregivers. Thank you for your healing Spirit.

May 3

The inhabitants of the villages ceased,
they ceased in Israel, until that I Deborah arose,
that I arose a mother in Israel.

—Judges 5:7

Thank you for those women who lead and guide and teach at church and in my community. These faithful women are excellent examples in how to serve you. Please grant your blessings upon them and help them grow ever more deeply in their love for you.

May 4

*L*ord, thank you for play and recreation. Drawing chalk pictures on the sidewalk with kids or grandkids, going hiking with a friend, or being part of a craft circle are all opportunities to rest, relax, and enjoy.

May 5

And Hannah answered and said,
No, my lord, I am a woman of a sorrowful spirit:
I have drunk neither wine nor strong drink,
but have poured out my soul before the Lord.

—1 Samuel 1:15

*L*ord, please send your comfort to those women who are struggling with infertility. Send your Spirit to console those parents who have suffered through the terrible pain of a miscarriage or the death of their child. Give those who are close to them words of gentleness and kindness, words that relieve pain instead of increasing it. Thank you for giving comfort even in times of desolation.

May 6

The days are getting longer, and everyone seems to be outside. Please keep my neighbors safe: the kids racing bicycles down the street, the friends playing tennis at the park, and the couple walking through the neighborhood. Thank you for this sense of shared joy and community we have as the days grow longer.

May 7

For the beauty of each hour

Of the day and of the night,

Hill and vale, and tree and flower,

Sun and moon and stars of light:

Christ, our God, to Thee we raise

This our Sacrifice of Praise.

Folliot Sandford Pierpoint,
"For the Beauty of the Earth"

May 8

Today I ask your blessing on those family, friends, neighbors, and members of my church community who are pregnant. Send your guardian angels to guard parents and child during the pregnancy and birth. Thank you for these new additions to our circle. I can't wait to meet them!

May 9

Sometimes I have a good chat with a good friend in which we cover every topic under the sun. Thank you for these long-standing friendships, where we know each other well and can be honest with one another. I am so grateful to have this person in my life.

May 10

And Jesus called a little child unto him,
and set him in the midst of them.

—Matthew 18:2

Watching a curious baby or toddler explore their world with wide eyes and open hands is a delight. They learn so much in such a short time. Lord, give them the gift of lifelong curiosity and wonder—and please grant it to me, too! Thank you.

May 11

She looketh well to the ways of her household,
and eateth not the bread of idleness.

—Proverbs 31:27

Lord, I can't say that I'm always happy to do my portion of the work of cleaning and maintaining a household. Dishes, bathrooms, carpets: why doesn't anything stay clean? When I'm feeling grouchy, let me remember to be thankful for shelter and for the pleasures of a clean home. Let me remember that the work isn't drudgework, but honorable. Making a comfortable home is work that's worth doing well.

May 12

Trust in the Lord with all thine heart;
and lean not unto thine own understanding.
In all thy ways acknowledge him,
and he shall direct thy paths.

—Proverbs 3:5–6

Sometimes the way forward seems muddled. I don't know how to make a decision, or I fear it's the wrong one. During those times, let me trust in you and truly  listen in order to discern your will. I can't see the full path ahead of me—I just need to trust that you'll be with me on it, guiding me at every step.

May 13

Thank you for endings:

The success of a project,

The child's graduation,

Our family's evening meal.

Thank you for each day's close:

Work set aside,

Dusk turning into night,

Peaceful rest and dreams.

May 14

Then Naomi her mother in law said unto her,
My daughter, shall I not seek rest for thee,
that it may be well with thee?

—Ruth 3:1

Thank you for those women who have acted as teachers and models to me, as godmother, grandmother, auntie, or mother-in-law. Please grant healing to any of those relationships that are flawed, and blessings on all these women who have shared wisdom and knowledge with me.

May 15

Cast me not off in the time of old age;
forsake me not when my strength faileth.

—Psalm 71:9

The aging process is not kind. When I see those I love struggle to find words, or notice that they are having trouble getting around, I grieve. When I see signs of aging in myself, sometimes I'm fearful. Let me remember with gratitude that we are all in your hands, in all the stages of our lives. You will not forsake us, loving God.

May 16

Yea, she reacheth forth her hands to the needy.

—Proverbs 31:20

Thank you for those whose vocation is serving the needs of others, including nurses, caregivers, social workers, and staff at assisted living facilities. Grant them patience and strength in dealing with the needs of their charges, and knowledge and discernment in untangling the demands of bureaucracy.

May 17

For the word of God is quick, and powerful,
and sharper than any twoedged sword,
piercing even to the dividing asunder of soul and spirit,
and of the joints and marrow, and is a discerner
of the thoughts and intents of the heart.

—Hebrews 4:12

Lord, you know that sometimes, through thoughtlessness or laziness or lack of care, I'm about to step astray. And then I open your Word and see a Bible verse that sets me on the right path again. Thank you for your help in turning away from the things that displease you.

May 18

Thank you for the gift of good memories. They are a comfort during difficult times and a source of joy during happier times.

When I remember negative things, help me to let go of any bitterness than remains. Holding onto grudges is one of those habits that can feel good at first, but it sours over time.

May 19

*For whatsoever things were written aforetime were
written for our learning, that we through patience
and comfort of the scriptures might have hope.*

—Romans 15:4

Thank you for
books and stories. I'm
grateful for writing that
informs, entertains,
and teaches me your
ways. Send your
inspiration to writers
and storytellers, that
they may tell their
stories with honesty
and truth.

May 20

But go ye and learn what that meaneth,
I will have mercy, and not sacrifice: for I am not come
to call the righteous, but sinners to repentance.

—Matthew 9:13

You know I am not perfect. I slip into sin, in big ways and in small. I lose my temper, or gossip, or make some remark that's clever but also cruel. Yet when I turn to you in repentance, I do so with the assurance of mercy. Thank you, forgiving God.

May 21

Then the twelve called the multitude of the disciples unto them, and said, It is not reason that we should leave the word of God, and serve tables. Wherefore, brethren, look ye out among you seven men of honest report, full of the Holy Ghost and wisdom, whom we may appoint over this business.

—Acts 6:2–3

Saying no can be difficult. When someone wants me to serve on a committee or take on a new volunteer opportunity, I don't want to miss a chance at serving you by not answering a call. At the same time, I don't want to be overextended or to be led away from the work that you are calling me to do because I find it difficult to say no to something else. Thank you for the gift of discernment that lets me know which choice to make and the courage to say no when I need to.

May 22

The light of the body is the eye:
if therefore thine eye be single,
thy whole body shall be full of light.

—Matthew 6:22

Thank you for the gift of sight! Thank you for all the beautiful things we can see: the vast array of colors, a new baby's smile, a rock flecked with glints of quartz. Help me keep my vision, physical and spiritual, focused on the things that are from you.

May 23

Thank you for the sense of hearing. Thank you for instrumental music and singing, laughter and conversation. Thank you for the purr of a satisfied cat, the hum of the air conditioner that means that all is running well, and the voice of a distant loved one over the phone or computer.

Let me use this sense both to truly listen to others and to listen to Your Word.

May 24

*And the house of Israel called the name thereof Manna
. . . and the taste of it was like wafers of honey.*

—Exodus 16:31

Thank you for the
sense of taste, for
blackberries picked
off the bush and
sashimi arranged
neatly on a plate, the
tartness of lemonade
and the flavor of good
coffee. Thank you for
the wide variety of
food we eat and the
cooks who prepare it.

May 25

The fig tree putteth forth her green figs,
and the vines with the tender grape give a good smell.
Arise, my love, my fair one, and come away.
                    —Song of Solomon 2:13

Thank you for the sense of smell: the scents of brownies baking, fresh-baked bread, newly-mowed grass, and crackling bonfires. Thank you for the smells that warn us that something is wrong, that there's a gas leak or a spot of mildew growing.

May 26

For she said within herself,
If I may but touch his garment, I shall be whole.
—Matthew 9:21

Thank you for the sense of touch: for flannel sheets in winter and a gentle breeze in summer, for the softness of a pet's fur and the smoothness of silk.

So many times in the Bible, Jesus heals through touch. Lord, let my touch be gentle when I express comfort through a hand held or a hug given.

May 27

The end of May and the beginning of June mark the end of the school year. Thanks for all that has been learned, and the teachers who strove to impart their knowledge. May your blessing be upon teachers and students as they go into summer break and enjoy their time away from the classroom!

For those students who graduated, please guide them on the next step of their journey.

May 28

I was a stranger, and ye took me in.

—Matthew 25:35

God, please keep those who are travelling this summer safe and healthy on their vacations. Let couples and families enjoy their time together. Let both the traveler in far lands and the people who encounter them see the face of God in each other.

Thank you for my own opportunities, for the chance to see your hand, Creating God, in different landscapes, and for the chance to worship among fellow believers who are strangers to me yet still brothers and sisters in faith.

May 29

Playing with a young child, one begins to see treasure in the simplest things. A pretty rock, a ball that bounces higher than the rest, and a fallen tree branch are all valuable and loved.

Thank you for the gift of simplicity.

May 30

The end of each May brings Memorial Day weekend. I am so grateful to those who chose to serve our country. We remember especially those who gave what Abraham Lincoln called "the last full measure of devotion."

May your comfort be with the families of those who passed away.

May 31

Thank you for those with an adventurous spirit—the people who try out new foods and new technologies and who come up with new inventions and ways of doing things. Thank you for those people who have the gift of creative inspiration, and who use it for the good of all of us!

June 1

*Honour thy father and mother; which is the first
commandment with promise; That it may be well
with thee, and thou mayest live long on the earth.
And, ye fathers, provoke not your children to wrath:
but bring them up in the nurture
and admonition of the Lord.*

—Ephesians 6:2–4

In this month of Father's Day, thank you for fathers!
Help all fathers provide what their children need and
teach them well as they move from infancy to adulthood.
Give wisdom to those stepfathers, foster fathers,
and adoptive fathers who are taking on a new role of
parenthood.

Thank you for my own father and all the memories we
share. I know you hold him in your hands always.

June 2

Be not afraid of their faces:
for I am with thee to deliver thee, saith the Lord.
Then the Lord put forth his hand,
and touched my mouth. And the Lord said unto me,
Behold, I have put my words in thy mouth.

—Jeremiah 1:8-9

Sometimes I flounder for words. But sometimes, when I am speaking your truth, I realize with amazement and gratitude that the right words are pouring out. So many of the people you chose to do your work were not eloquent by nature. Let me, like them, trust that you will give me the words I need.

June 3

*And the third day there was a marriage
in Cana of Galilee; and the mother of Jesus was there:
And both Jesus was called, and his disciples,
to the marriage.*

—John 2:1–2

In June, this month of frequent weddings, thank you for romantic and married love. Please bless those engaged couples in my extended family and community with a strong and lasting love and commitment. In these days of extravagant weddings, let us enjoy the communal celebrations with good cheer and without strife or undue stress.

June 4

*And the Lord went before them by day in a pillar
of a cloud, to lead them the way; and by night in a pillar
of fire, to give them light; to go by day and night.*

—Exodus 13:21

*L*ord, sometimes I am not sure what path to take.
Other time, you give very clear signs. Thank you
for those bright, blazing signs that lead me away
from danger, straight towards you.

June 5

*Ye are the children of the prophets, and of the covenant
which God made with our fathers, saying unto Abraham,
And in thy seed shall all the kindreds
of the earth be blessed.*

—Acts 3:25

Thank you for those men who serve you as leaders and
"fathers" of the community. Give them the courage of
Moses, the zeal of David, and the wisdom of Solomon.
Most of all, give them a loving and humble heart.

June 6

Now it came to pass, as they went,
that he entered into a certain village:
and a certain woman named Martha received him
into her house. And she had a sister called Mary,
which also sat at Jesus' feet, and heard his word.
But Martha was cumbered about much serving,
and came to him, and said, Lord, dost thou not care
that my sister hath left me to serve alone?
bid her therefore that she help me. And Jesus answered
and said unto her, Martha, Martha, thou art careful
and troubled about many things:
But one thing is needful: and Mary hath chosen
that good part, which shall not be taken away from her.

—Luke 10:38–42

$\mathcal{L}$ord, you know that I've played the roles of both Martha and Mary at different times in my life. Let me not be so busy with distractions and ideas of what need to be done that I forget to sit in your presence. When I am working and serving, let me do so cheerfully and without resentment.

June 7

And the angel of the Lord said unto him,
Wherefore hast thou smitten thine ass these three times?
behold, I went out to withstand thee, because thy way is
perverse before me: And the ass saw me,
and turned from me these three times:
unless she had turned from me,
surely now also I had slain thee, and saved her alive.
And Balaam said unto the angel of the Lord,
I have sinned.

—Numbers 22:32–34

Thank you for obstacles that turn out to be blessings!
When I'm running into stumbling blocks, please give
me the wisdom to know whether the path I'm on is
one worth pursuing despite difficulties—or whether
I'm being stubborn like Balaam, persisting despite the
angel standing in my way.

June 8

Give unto the Lord, O ye mighty,

give unto the Lord glory and strength.

Give unto the Lord the glory due unto his name;

worship the Lord in the beauty of holiness.

The voice of the Lord is upon the waters:

the God of glory thundereth:

The Lord is upon many waters.

The voice of the Lord is powerful;

the voice of the Lord is full of majesty.

—Psalm 29:1–4

June 9

$\mathcal{L}$ord, please bless new and expectant fathers. Ease their nervousness. Help new parents work together as a team. There's so much information out there— often conflicting—about how to raise children! Help parents sift through the advice they receive to find the things they truly need to know and do.

June 10

$\mathcal{I}$ pray today for those fathers who have lost children. Let the families and friends of those parents whose children have passed away be a strong support. May your Spirit bring comfort and healing. Thank you for your eternal presence.

$\mathcal{I}$ pray also for those who are estranged from their children. May your Spirit work to bring about understanding and reconciliation.

June 11

And the son said unto him, Father,
I have sinned against heaven, and in thy sight,
and am no more worthy to be called thy son.
But the father said to his servants,
Bring forth the best robe, and put it on him;
and put a ring on his hand, and shoes on his feet
—Luke 15:21–22

*F*ather God, for
those times when
I am estranged
from you, I ask
forgiveness. Thank
you for always
welcoming me
back with joy!

June 12

Now his elder son was in the field:
and as he came and drew nigh to the house,
he heard musick and dancing.
And he called one of the servants,
and asked what these things meant.

—Luke 15:25–26

I'm not immune to jealousy, and sometimes I find myself playing the role of envious Prodigal Brother. When I'm angry at or judgmental about someone else's spiritual journey, please remind me to keep my eyes on you, with gratitude for all you give me.

June 13

When I rise in the morning,

Let me praise you.

When I eat and drink,

Let me praise you.

On my journey to work,

Let me praise you.

When I am discouraged,

Let me praise you.

When we share the evening meal,

Let me praise you.

At the end of each day,

Let me praise you.

June 14

Thank you for the highlights of summer, the days of swimming pools, picnics, fireflies, and butterflies. Keep us safe this summer as we appreciate visits from the ice cream truck, sandcastles, and hazy summer evenings spent in the backyard.

June 15

*L*aughter is truly contagious. Sometimes at a meeting or over a family dinner, someone will say something that will set all of us off into fits of unstoppable giggles. We return to conversation with loosened muscles and better spirits. Thank you for the gift of laughter!

June 16

Even a child is known by his doings,
whether his work be pure, and whether it be right.

—Proverbs 20:11

Thank you for diligence. It is satisfying to finish work and know that it is done well. Help me give my work, whether paid or volunteer or in the house, the attention it deserves.

At the same time, when I do make a mistake, help me not be such a perfectionist that I won't forgive myself!

June 17

When I consider thy heavens, the work of thy fingers,
the moon and the stars, which thou hast ordained;
What is man, that thou art mindful of him?

—Psalm 8:3–4

When I think about the size of the universe, it's staggering. Your creation is so grand, God of all! Yet you care about our small concerns. Like a child who trusts that her parents will listen to her everyday triumphs and concerns, let me trust in you.

June 18

And Moses' father in law said unto him,
The thing that thou doest is not good.
Thou wilt surely wear away, both thou,
and this people that is with thee:
for this thing is too heavy for thee;
thou art not able to perform it thyself alone.
Hearken now unto my voice, I will give thee counsel,
and God shall be with thee.

—Exodus 18:17–19

*E*xodus tells the story of Jethro, Moses' father-in-law, giving him concrete advice on how to avoid burnout. Thank you, God, for all those who have acted in the role of father to me, both the father who raised me and those father-figures, grandfathers, uncles, and mentors who have taken the time to give me wise and thoughtful counsel.

June 19

For ye have not received the spirit of bondage again
to fear; but ye have received the Spirit of adoption,
whereby we cry, Abba, Father.

—Romans 8:15

Father God, how astonishing it is to me that I can turn to you for protection, for counsel, and for comfort! Sometimes I turn to you like a small child, bewildered by the injustices of the world, crying out that it's not fair. Sometimes I'm more like a teenager, returning to your arms after some act of rebellion. Sometimes I look back over my life and wonder at the gifts you've given me, like an adult remembering the care of her parents. As Jesus called you father, so can I—how amazing and wonderful that is!

June 20

But the fruit of the Spirit is love, joy, peace,
longsuffering, gentleness, goodness, faith, meekness,
temperance: against such there is no law.

—Galatians 5:22–23

*L*ord, thank you for your Spirit. Let me be open
to your Spirit so that I will produce "good fruit."

June 21

Though I speak with the tongues of men and of angels,
and have not charity, I am become as sounding brass,
or a tinkling cymbal. And though I have the gift
of prophecy, and understand all mysteries,
and all knowledge; and though I have all faith,
so that I could remove mountains, and have not charity,
I am nothing. And though I bestow all my goods
to feed the poor, and though I give my body to be burned,
and have not charity, it profiteth me nothing.
—1 Corinthians 13:1–3

Lord, lead me always not just to take the "right" actions, but to do them with love. I don't want to be someone whose generosity comes with a dose of harsh judgment, whose advice comes with a side of condescension. Thank you for those who have truly modeled your love to me.

June 22

But let all those that put their trust in thee rejoice:
let them ever shout for joy, because thou defendest them:
let them also that love thy name be joyful in thee.

—Psalm 5:11

We know that we will go through desert times and difficulties, but we also have the assurance that your love brings joy. We see this over and  over in the Bible, as the exile returns home or God raises up a leader to champion the forsaken. We see this in Jesus' death and resurrection. God of joy, thank you!

June 23

And into whatsoever house ye enter, first say,
Peace be to this house.

—Luke 10:5

Thank you for the gift of peace. I find peace in the knowledge that the right decision has been made, in the stillness of sitting in silence and prayer, and in the calm moments amidst a busy day. Let me be an instrument of your peace, bringing it to others.

June 24

The Lord is not slack concerning his promise,
as some men count slackness; but is longsuffering
to us-ward, not willing that any should perish,
but that all should come to repentance.

—2 Peter 3:9

*L*ord, thank you for your longsuffering patience. You
know that sometimes it takes me a few tries to understand
your will for me. Sometimes I get impatient in my turn,
seeing so clearly what someone else
should do, and I get almost angry
when they do not heed my advice. It's
easy to think that if they only listened
to me, they would save themselves
some trouble! But impatience
and pushiness will only create a
rift between us. Let me instead be
patient with them as you are with me.

June 25

And the servant of the Lord must not strive;
but be gentle unto all men, apt to teach, patient,
In meekness instructing those that oppose themselves.
—2 Timothy 2:24–25

Lord, thank you for those who have been examples of gentleness for me on my faith journey, and who have been gentle with me as they taught me. Sometimes even if someone has the right answers, we're turned away if they seem holier-than-thou or smarter-than-thou. Thank you for those people who guide by example instead.

June 26

But ye are a chosen generation, a royal priesthood, a holy nation, a peculiar people; that ye should shew forth the praises of him who hath called you out of darkness into his marvellous light.

—1 Peter 2:9

*L*et me seek to do what is good and right in your eyes, God. Let me do so even when it's difficult. Thank you for those times you've given me the courage to make the good choice, even if it hasn't been popular.

June 27

O Lord, thou art my God; I will exalt thee,
I will praise thy name;
for thou hast done wonderful things;
thy counsels of old are faithfulness and truth.

—Isaiah 25:1

Lord, thank you for your steadfast faithfulness to me. Guide me to be faithful in return. That doesn't mean just keeping your commandments or trying not to sin. It means taking time to pray and build a relationship with you. It means putting you at the center of my life.

June 28

Brethren, if a man be overtaken in a fault,
ye which are spiritual, restore such an one in the spirit
of meekness; considering thyself,
lest thou also be tempted.

—Galatians 6:1

*H*umility can be a hard virtue to put into practice. We sometimes fall into a strange and boastful competition to prove that someone's worse than us: "I may be a sinner, but at least I don't do *that!*" When I'm in that mindset, let me remember the parable of the Pharisee and the publican. Thank you for those who have corrected me in a spirit of humility and meekness.

June 29

Hast thou found honey? eat so much as is sufficient
for thee, lest thou be filled therewith, and vomit it.

—Proverbs 25:16

Lord, please give me a spirit of temperance and self-control. Help me to keep from over-indulging—in food, in anger, in lust, in bragging, or in exercise. Thank you for your help.

June 30

And beside this, giving all diligence,
add to your faith virtue; and to virtue knowledge;
And to knowledge temperance;
and to temperance patience; and to patience godliness;
And to godliness brotherly kindness;
and to brotherly kindness charity.

—2 Peter 1:5–7

Lord, where I'm
imperfect, please forgive
my imperfections.
Where I'm striving for
virtue, please help me.
Where I'm succeeding,
let me not be boastful or
proud. Help me grow to
love you with my whole
heart and soul.

July 1

We don't really know why we have to get sick, Lord. We only know your promise: No matter where we are or what we are called to endure, there you are in the midst of it with us, never leaving our side. Not for a split second. Thank you, Lord of all.

July 2

A friend loveth at all times,
and a brother is born for adversity.

—Proverbs 17:17

$\mathcal{O}$ur sisters and our brothers mean so much to us. They give when we need their strength and listen when we need their help. Sometimes a simple "thank you" is the most powerful message of love we can send to our siblings. It says so much more than we could hope to articulate.

July 3

I will speak of the glorious honour of thy majesty,
and of thy wondrous works.

—Psalm 145:5

*L*ord, I can hear your voice in the bubbling brook, see your beauty in the petals of a flower, and feel your gentle breath in the evening breeze and in the soft kiss of a child. Thank you for all of these gifts.

July 4

I exhort therefore, that, first of all, supplications,
prayers, intercessions, and giving of thanks,
be made for all men; For kings, and for all that are
in authority; that we may lead a quiet
and peaceable life in all godliness and honesty.

—1 Timothy 2:1–2

Thank you for my country, and all the blessings we have.
Please help our leaders guide this country wisely and well.
Bless all those
who serve to
keep our country
safe and do the
work to keep our
country running.

July 5

$\mathcal{I}$ remember it—coming from a swim and lying back in white sand—the gift of a moment to rest, to sit in reverie, to watch, to close eyes and think of nothing but the sound of breaking waves. Yes, you were there with the sounds and the sunshine, and I am thankful.

July 6

Friends give so much to me—

a listening ear

a soothing voice

a caring heart

a helping hand

a healing hug

a cheering smile.

Thank you for all my loving friends.

July 7

*And the Lord answered me, and said, Write the vision,
and make it plain upon tables,
that he may run that readeth it.*

—Habakkuk 2:2

$\mathcal{S}$ome people have the ability to write words that lift
the heart and soothe the soul. Let's thank God for
those who serve us in this way.

July 8

*That ye may be the children of your Father
which is in heaven: for he maketh his sun to rise
on the evil and on the good, and sendeth rain
on the just and on the unjust.*

—Matthew 5:45

*B*e thankful for all of creation. Embrace the hope of each new morning and the last ray of sunshine to fall at day's end.

July 9

God, when things go wrong, we often blame you
first. Forgive us for even considering that you would
deliberately hurt one of your very own children.
What could you possibly have to gain? Thank you for
your presence, and please forgive our many sins.

July 10

Thank God when the pain ends, when once again we're well and whole and strong. Thank God when our bodies are released from the blinding, mind-numbing hurts that affect our whole lives. Thank God when we have complete victory over pain.

July 11

For I was an hungred, and ye gave me meat:
I was thirsty, and ye gave me drink: I was a stranger,
and ye took me in: Naked, and ye clothed me: I was sick,
and ye visited me: I was in prison, and ye came unto me.
—Matthew 25:35–36

Thank you, Lord, for helping us through our hard times. You have shown your love for us and made us more compassionate people. Help us show the same love to others who are going through hard times.

July 12

I prayed for an angel to comfort me at night.

I prayed for an angel to make the darkness bright.

When the long night was over and the pain was all gone,

I thanked God for the angel who kept me safe until dawn.

July 13

God, help me to accept the help I need and to give up my stubborn need to control the outcome of every situation. Show me that sometimes my will is not always the best and that sometimes you send us helping angels in the form of other humans. Thank you.

July 14

Thou shalt neither vex a stranger, nor oppress him:
for ye were strangers in the land of Egypt.

—Exodus 22:21

God Almighty, thank you for the people that inspire
me to accept others. Let me learn to love everyone—
including myself.

July 15

$\mathcal{H}$eavenly Father, it is good to remember that everything that lives and breathes is sacred to you. We must never feel superior to any other human being, for we are all precious in your eyes. You have given us life, and we must make the choices that lead to kindness and peace. You created us, but how we live together is up to us. Thank you.

July 16

But Jesus turned him about, and when he saw her,
he said, Daughter, be of good comfort;
thy faith hath made thee whole.

—Matthew 9:22

God, thank you for letting me cling to the faith that has sustained me through so much uncertainty and pain before. I now know that although faith may be all I have, it's also all I need.

July 17

Thank you for the unseen hands that guide my way.

Thank you for the eyes that watch my step.

Thank you for the care that keeps me safe,

even when the angels are incognito.

Thank you for the trouble I have missed even though

I never saw it coming. Every visible thing

in the world is under the charge of an angel.

—Saint Augustine

July 18

$\mathcal{P}$ardon my muddy feet, God of raindrops and wriggle worms. I've been outside. Splashing in puddles like a child does to rediscover your creation: cloak of fog, spiderweb weavings, birds of different feathers dining peacefully together. I get too busy to enjoy it. Thank you for this muddy day when I am brought to my knees in awe, the best place to meet you—as any child knows.

July 19

Lord God, I kneel before you, and you alone.

I'm sorry for the times I've mistakenly

Credited someone else or something else

For your miraculous work.

How could an angel, a preacher, a friend

Impart your healing power, unless

You were behind it all,

Inspiring, instructing, empowering?

I thank you for the ones you use

On this earth and in your heaven

To help me heal.

Lord God, I kneel before you, and you alone.

July 20

A man that hath friends must shew himself friendly:
and there is a friend that sticketh closer than a brother.

—Proverbs 18:24

Thank God for the friends who lift you up when you feel low; they share the weight when your own load is too heavy to bear.

July 21

Thank you, Lord, for good marriages. Like a wedding band, love between spouses circles but doesn't bind. In your grace, married love has the permanence of rock, not of walls, but of a bridge to moments ahead as special and bright as when the couple first met.

July 22

So teach us to number our days,
that we may apply our hearts unto wisdom.

—Psalm 90:12

Thank you for the grandparents who tended us so well. Bless these bigger-than-life companions who helped us bridge home and away, childhood and maturity. In their footsteps, we made the journey. Thank you for the heritage they passed along.

July 23

*Wherefore, if God so clothe the grass of the field,
which to day is, and to morrow is cast into the oven,
shall he not much more clothe you, O ye of little faith?*
—Matthew 6:30

Bless this roof over our heads, and keep it from leaking. But more than that, move us to give thanks for the next rainstorm. Because you are more than a good roof—we need to remember that. And our neighbors' crops need watering more than we need to stay dry.

July 24

$\mathcal{I}$t is good, dear God, to be a part of this family: circle of love, place of rest, bastion of peace. When every other source of comfort fails, this is where I return. Thank you for being in our midst.

July 25

Thank you for the gift of memory. Playing "I remember" is such fun, Lord of history, especially the sharing of it with children and grandchildren, nieces and nephews, who, like relay runners, are here to pick up their part of our family tale.

July 26

*H*ow good it is to be recognized for hard work! I thank you for the chance to savor it. A job well done is a good thing, I know. I will celebrate before your smiling eyes and give you credit, too. Because, after all, everything I am and have comes from your gracious hand.

July 27

Thank you, God, for the wisdom to know when to speak, what to say, and how to say it. Guard my mouth today from any form of foolishness, that in all circumstances I might honor you with my words.

July 28

Delight thyself also in the Lord:
and he shall give thee the desires of thine heart.

—Psalm 37:4

Thank you for the
funny bone, Lord,
placed next to hearts
broken by anxiety
and fear. A good belly
laugh is a gift from
you, expanding and
healing heart, lungs,
and mind.

July 29

God, a call, a note, and a handclasp from a friend are simple and seemingly insignificant. Yet you inspire these gifts from people we have a special affection for. These cherished acts of friendship nudge aside doubts about who we are when we feel low and encourage our hearts in a way that lifts our spirits. Thank you for the friends you have given us.

July 30

*D*ear God, isn't it funny how much better I feel when I choose to love? And yet how many times in the course of my life have I chosen anger or hatred or fear? Let me always choose love first, for when I do make that choice, it opens up the doorway to new friendships and joy that other choices cannot give me. Make love be not only my first choice but my only choice. Thank you, God, for choosing to love me.

July 31

God, I feel happy today, and I have you to thank for that. No matter what is going on outside of me, I am strong and safe and secure inside because you love and care for me. Thank you for loving me when I have been cranky, tired, lazy, and even mean. Thank you for being there when I ignored your presence, God. Your steadfast love is a constant reminder of just how good I have it in life. And that makes me happiest of all!

August 1

Thou hast set all the borders of the earth:
thou hast made summer and winter.

—Psalm 74:17

Thank you for this
new month. We're
in the late days of
summer now, trying to
pack in everything we
want to do before the
cooler weather arrives.
Thank you for the
busy days and the lazy
days as we progress
through this season.

August 2

There are people who just rub me the wrong way. Even when I think they're in the right about something or know they mean well, something about their attitude just gets under my skin.

Lord, keep me calm and kind when I interact with those people. Let me remember that they, like me, were made in your image. Let me even by thankful about their presence in my life, for it teaches me patience and compassion.

August 3

And withal they learn to be idle, wandering around from house to house; and not only idle, but tattlers also and busybodies, speaking things which they ought not.

—1 Timothy 5:13

Unfortunately, even church communities aren't immune to gossip. Lord, when I hear it, please give me the strength to speak up and put a stop to it. When I fall into it myself, please let me realize it and stop. When I'm the subject of gossip, please let me take it in stride, and let my behavior be without blemish. Thank you.

August 4

Lord, I never imagined when I was young that growing older could be such a blessing. The experience and the wisdom I have now about how life works—these are gifts I would never trade for anything. Some people dread their later years, but mine are so blessed—I can only imagine how good the rest of my days will be. Thank you, Lord, for allowing me the privilege of getting older.

August 5

Bless the Lord, ye his angels, that excel in strength,
that do his commandments,
hearkening unto the voice of his word.

—Psalm 103:20

Father, the wind rustling the leaves reminds me of angel wings all around me. Thank you for such a reminder. Help me stay mindful that the work of angels goes on all the time all around me whether I am aware or not, and that life is even more than I see.

August 6

Thank you for cool things, Lord: sprinklers for the kids to run through, pitchers of iced tea, ceiling fans and air conditioners that hum busily. Thank you for cooler evenings after long, sweltering days, shade trees that break up a walk in the sun, and cool, fresh water after a long drive.

August 7

Therefore, brethren, stand fast,
and hold the traditions which ye have been taught,
whether by word, or our epistle.

—2 Thessalonians 2:15

We're caught up
in well-worn, comfy
traditions, Lord.
Keep them worthy,
for like a deer path
through the forest,
they lead us forward
and back. Thank you
for the divine love
and holiness found
in the ordinary.

August 8

*L*ord, please help all those who are going through a divorce. Please be with both people as they separate their lives and create new routines and new ways of life. Help them keep a spirit of fairness and civility. Where there are children involved, be with those children and give them peace and surety in troubled times. Thank you.

August 9

That every man should eat and drink, and enjoy the good of all his labour, it is the gift of God.

—Ecclesiastes 3:13

Thank you for the unexpected! Thank you for the distant friend passing through town on travel, the surprise bonus, the last-minute tickets to an event. Thank you for spontaneity and serendipity.

August 10

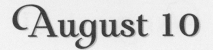

My closest friends, dear Lord, are a reprieve for my soul. Their acceptance sets me free to be myself. Their unconditional love forgives my failings. Thank you for these people who are a reflection of your love in my life. Help me be a friend who will lay down my life in such loving ways.

August 11

$\mathcal{L}$ord, please help the entrepreneurs and business owners in our communities who bring new stores and restaurants that add variety to our neighborhood. Please guide them to deal honestly and fairly with their customers. Grant them calm during times of financial stress. Thank you for all those who value hard work and new ideas!

August 12

Geese take turns, take up the slack, in the natural rhythm of things. By sharing our journey, we, too, gain that updraft of air, where we'll rest awhile. Thank you for those who give support—those who babysit one child when parents are busy dealing with their other child's health crisis, who act as respite caregivers for the elderly, who volunteer to serve on a church committee while a new mother focuses on her kids. Thank you for those who have given me support during my "resting" periods, so I could return to serve you, refreshed and invigorated.

August 13

And to love him with all the heart,
and with all the understanding, and with all the soul,
and with all the strength,
and to love his neighbour as himself,
is more than all whole burnt offerings and sacrifices.

—Mark 12:33

One of life's greatest
sorrows is love that is
not returned. One of
life's greatest joys is
knowing that someone
loves me and is willing
to complete the circle
of love. Thank you for
the great gift of love,
beginning always with
your love.

August 14

Be of good courage, and he shall strengthen your heart,
all ye that hope in the Lord.

—Psalm 31:24

Hope is the soul's faithful friend, holding its hand through the night and saying, "There will be a glorious dawn." To live in hope means to expect that our longings will be fulfilled. When we hold that image of fulfillment constantly, we cannot help but notice all the ways in which our lives are blessed.

August 15

When the darkness casts shadows upon us

and the answers are nowhere in sight,

hope lifts us up on a wing and a prayer

and carries us back to the light.

August 16

And Jesus said unto him, Go thy way;
thy faith hath made thee whole. And immediately
he received his sight, and followed Jesus in the way.

—Mark 10:52

Faith empowers me to leap across the chasms in my life and to have the confidence that I'll make it to the other side—and to believe that the other side exists. Thank you for the gift of faith.

August 17

Now when this was noised abroad,
the multitude came together, and were confounded,
because that every man heard them speak
in his own language. And they were all amazed
and marvelled, saying one to another, Behold,
are not all these which speak Galilaeans?

—Acts 2:6–7

Color outside the lines of ordinary life, following the vision of life that God has in mind; you'll be amazed at the portrait that emerges. Like the disciples who spread the gospel in the days of the early church, your life will be transformed.

August 18

If ye have faith as a grain of mustard seed,
ye shall say unto this mountain,
Remove hence to yonder place; and it shall remove;
and nothing shall be impossible unto you.

—Matthew 17:20

I will not let the
pessimists of the
world squelch my
belief that what
I do can make
a difference. I
am determined
to maintain my
inspiration to change
the world in whatever
small ways I can.

August 19

A wise teacher shows students not what to do but how to do things. One who is taught how to learn develops a skill that is useful throughout life.

As the school year approaches, grant wisdom to teachers and curiosity and diligence to students. Thank you for those teachers who were inspirations to me!

August 20

Thank you not only for teachers but for all those who work to keep students safe and learning: the bus drivers, crossing guards, cafeteria workers, janitors, administrators, and assistants. Help the interactions they have with students be positive for both sides.

August 21

The hope of the righteous shall be gladness:
but the expectation of the wicked shall perish.

—Proverbs 10:28

Thank you for those in my life who have hoped for and expected good things from me. Those expectations have given me something to work towards. Please help me forgive those who had unrealistic expectations, who put unhelpful pressure on me in difficult times.

August 22

We glory in tribulations also:
knowing that tribulation worketh patience;
And patience, experience; and experience, hope.
—Romans 5:3–4

Lord, sometimes I
wish for more patience.
Then I realize that, as
I wade my way through
the difficulties life is
throwing at me, I'm
slowly developing the
virtue of patience.
Even if I'm not always
grateful at the time, I'm
grateful afterwards for
the way virtues can grow
under pressure.

August 23

Thank you for good neighbors, those who are willing to collect mail and lend a pair of hedge clippers. Where there is conflict between neighbors, please ease it. Give people patience and clear vision when they are dealing with problems caused by misunderstandings rather than malice or ill will.

August 24

Lord, sometimes we become entrenched in our roles. We're known or know others by only one characteristic—that woman is the organized one; that man is the one with the hot temper. Please deepen our understanding of each other so that we see more than just one-dimensional portraits. Maybe we'll realize that we've been overlooking someone's creative talent, their compassion, or their ability to lead. Thank you.

August 25

At church, sometimes there are people who have been leaders in some capacity for a long time—and it's time for them to step away from that role. It can be difficult for everyone. Please help those who lead know when it is time for them to step aside and pave the way for a new direction. Please help all of us honor those who have served well in positions of leadership. Thank you.

August 26

When our lives get overloaded, one of the first things we cut back is the time we spend with friends. But it is these very relationships that can center us, ease our stress, and remind us of our true priorities. Thank you for those who make time for me. Please help me do the same.

August 27

We often hesitate to extend help unless asked. We don't want to interfere or overstep our boundaries, or we are afraid that our behavior will be misinterpreted. But an opportunity to assist others is a rare gift, and if your actions come from the heart, you will never be misjudged. Thank you for those who have offered help to me when they saw I was struggling with something, even if I was too afraid or proud to reach out first.

August 28

*Wherefore comfort yourselves together,
and edify one another, even as also ye do.*
—1 Thessalonians 5:11

Knowing he needs encouragement, I pray for my friend, Lord. Lifting my heart to you on his behalf, may I not fail, either, to reach my hand to his—just as you are holding mine.

August 29

*But as they sailed he fell asleep: and there came down
a storm of wind on the lake; and they were filled with
water, and were in jeopardy. And they came to him, and
awoke him, saying, Master, master, we perish. Then he
arose, and rebuked the wind and the raging of the water;
and they ceased, and there was a calm.*

—Luke 8:23–24

Storms sometimes
arrive in our lives with
hurricane-force winds.
We feel as if our hearts are
caught in the vortex. But
just when we think we'll
be destroyed, a still, small
voice appears in the eye
of the storm to remind us
that we are not alone.

August 30

*And the Lord said unto him, I have heard thy prayer
and thy supplication, that thou hast made before me:
I have hallowed this house, which thou hast built,
to put my name there for ever; and mine eyes
and mine heart shall be there perpetually.*

—1 Kings 9:3

Thank you for calling
me to prayer, Lord.
In the midst of other
things, I'll be reminded
that I haven't spoken
about the problem
to you. When I panic
about a problem, I feel
infinitely better once
I've carried the problem
to you in prayer.

August 31

By this shall all men know that ye are my disciples,
if ye have love one to another.

—John 13:35

We reflect the goodness of God most when we love others. It is life's highest, and sometimes most difficult, goal. Thank you for calling us to love.

September 1

One of the hardest things about loving someone is when we must helplessly watch them make wrong decisions and learn life's lessons the hard way. Every parent knows the ache of watching the children we love make foolish choices. Lord, please help us all remember to return to your loving arms when we have stumbled. Help me to be compassionate, not judgmental, about the choices of others, remembering with gratitude those who have responded with compassion to me.

September 2

*Yea, all of you be subject one to another,
and be clothed with humility: for God resisteth
the proud, and giveth grace to the humble.*

—1 Peter 5:5

Like a multifaceted stone, the humble person's colors shine forth. By their nature, they are able to bear an injustice without retaliating, do their duty even when they are not watched, keep at the job until it is finished, and make use of criticism without being defeated by it. Thank you, Lord, for those who model humility.

September 3

But sanctify the Lord God in your hearts:
and be ready always to give an answer to every man that
asketh you a reason of the hope
that is in you with meekness and fear.

—1 Peter 3:15

When we attempt to explain our faith to others, it may not help them—or we may not see the results for some time—but it can assist us in understanding why we believe and what weak spots exist in our faith. Thank you for those conversations that might have seemed like challenges at the time.

September 4

Thank you for those who labor, for those who attend to their work with diligence. Thank you for those colleagues who pitch in without complaint when we're up against a deadline. Thank you for senior colleagues who have mentored me when I was new at a job. Thank you for new colleagues who bring fresh perspectives to the work we do.

September 5

My brethren, count it all joy when ye fall into divers temptations; Knowing this, that the trying of your faith worketh patience. But let patience have her perfect work, that ye may be perfect and entire, wanting nothing.

—James 1:2–4

If our faith was never tested, how would we know we had any? When things go wrong and we can still say, "I believe in God no matter what happens," we show our faith to be real.

September 6

God, I know you're not in a hurry—
Your plans for me are on time.
You need no schedule or reminders
For I'm always on your mind.

I know you have drawn the mosaic
And you're fitting each tile in place.
As I continue to follow your plan,
Help me not to hurry or race.

So as my life's pattern continues
And the next part begins to unfold,
It's you I'm thanking and praising,
It's your hand I cling to and hold.

September 7

We all prefer to deal with honest people—people we can trust—people who will not lie or try to deceive us. A noble goal for one's life is to pursue honesty: honesty with others, with ourselves, and with God. Yet it is hard to tell the truth. Honesty can seem to leave us open to attack—to tear down the walls of protection we would rather erect in our lives. Scripture tells us, "The truth shall make you free." Although it might be hard to be honest, if we do it with loving intentions, the burden that dishonesty brings will be lifted. Thank you, Lord, for the freedom that comes from living one's life honestly.

September 8

Moreover if thy brother shall trespass against thee,
go and tell him his fault between thee and him alone:
if he shall hear thee, thou hast gained thy brother.

—Matthew 18:15

Though we may feel noble when we brutally tell people the truth about their faults, we need to be honest about our own faults first. After we've done that, our honesty becomes gentler. Thank you for those who have corrected me with gentleness.

September 9

And above all things have fervent charity among
yourselves: for charity shall cover the multitude of sins.

—1 Peter 4:8

Even if we feel we've been wronged by someone, if
we soften our hearts and forgive the one who wronged
us, the burden of bitterness will be lifted. This change
is certain to affect the lives of those around us.

September 10

Let integrity and uprightness preserve me;
for I wait on thee.

—Psalm 25:21

Do we prize integrity above the tangible things in life? Are we concerned with being what we say we are? To become a person of integrity is a high calling and one worth pursuing. Thank you, Father God, for those who have modeled integrity for me.

September 11

*Thank you for your love that encompasses us
in times of trial.*

*Thank you for those who bravely walk
into danger to help others.*

Thank you for memories that comfort.

September 12

But be ye doers of the word, and not hearers only,
deceiving your own selves. For if any be a hearer
of the word, and not a doer, he is like unto a man
beholding his natural face in a glass:
For he beholdeth himself, and goeth his way,
and straightway forgetteth what manner of man he was.

—James 1:22–24

We've all heard that "actions speak louder than words."
And so it is with the Christian life. Like it or not, we
affect others by what we say and do. Whether with friends,
 family, coworkers, or even
total strangers, God wants
us to always treat others
with the utmost care and
respect. Thank you, Lord,
for helping me to act
with integrity.

September 13

We who consider ourselves the Lord's servants sometimes have a hard time receiving from others. Although Jesus said, "It's more blessed to give than receive," this statement also says, "it is blessed to receive." Thank you for those people who have reached out to offer help even when I've been stubbornly silent.

September 14

When we remember that we are working for the rewards of heaven and not for the praise of people, we are able to press on and persevere in the tasks ahead of us. Lord, please give me a steadfast and grateful heart in the face of adversity.

September 15

*And Miriam the prophetess, the sister of Aaron,
took a timbrel in her hand; and all the women went out
after her with timbrels and with dances.*

—Exodus 15:20

Thank you for the gift of dance, from a child skipping along and making up her own steps to the first dance of a couple at their wedding. Cultures throughout the world have used dance to express joy. In fact, God's word commands us to dance as an expression of worship and joy.

September 16

Either what woman having ten pieces of silver,
if she lose one piece, doth not light a candle,
and sweep the house, and seek diligently till she find it?
And when she hath found it, she calleth her friends
and her neighbours together, saying, Rejoice with me;
for I have found the piece which I had lost. Likewise,
I say unto you, there is joy in the presence of the angels
of God over one sinner that repenteth.

—Luke 15:8–10

There is great joy when lost things are found—lost lambs, lost coins, but especially lost people. Sometimes we lose our joy, like the older brother in the story of the prodigal son. The good news is that we can turn to God and find it again. Thank you for all that I have lost and found again!

September 17

*Again, the kingdom of heaven is like unto treasure hid
in a field; the which when a man hath found, he hideth,
and for joy thereof goeth and selleth all that he hath,
and buyeth that field.*

—Matthew 13:44

We all want to be
happy, but joy goes
much deeper. Joy is not
based on circumstances
or feelings, which
change like the weather.
True joy comes from a
celebration of the heart
over the things that do
not change—things that
come from God.

September 18

Glory to God in the highest, and on earth peace,
good will toward men.

—Luke 2:14

The wonder of your peace is that even when the world around us is in confusion and our emotions are in a whirl, underneath it all we can know your peace. Thank you, Prince of Peace!

September 19

I will say of the Lord, He is my refuge and my fortress:
my God; in him will I trust.

—Psalm 91:2

God shelters his people in the short term and rewards them in the long term. He uses his strength as a refuge for those who trust him. I praise your name, loving God.

September 20

If it be possible, as much as lieth in you,
live peaceably with all men.

—Romans 12:18

$\mathcal{L}$ord, I need you here in the midst of this difficult situation, that the very warmth of your love will bring about the resolution and that the brightness of your light will cast out all shadows between us. Thank you.

September 21

God, I know that you close some doors in my life in order to open new ones. I know that things change and come to an end in order to leave room for new beginnings. Help me have the boldness and enthusiasm to let go of the old and accept the new. Thank you for new beginnings.

September 22

$\mathcal{T}$he days are getting a little shorter and a little colder. Thank you for this season of autumn, for the beauty of trees that are changing color and the warmth of apple cider. Thank you for the foods of fall, roasted vegetables and butternut squash. Thank you for the crunch of fallen leaves under our feet and the brisk breeze in our faces as we walk. Thank you for the cycle of seasons!

September 23

The sting of rejection lingers long after it has been inflicted. It often creates an aversion to drawing near to the very thing that can bring healing: love through a relationship with God. It takes a certain willingness to risk reaching out to be forgiven by God if we ever hope to find wholeness again. But there is no more worthwhile risk than that which risks for the sake of God's love.

Thank you, God, for welcoming us with open arms.

September 24

*L*ord, when times are dark and I feel like huddling
under the covers, I look up and see wings fluttering
against the window and know with gratitude that
a God who can make a butterfly from a caterpillar
can surely make something new of me.

September 25

After a frustrating day, a few minutes with a good book or a soul-renewing walk can give me a renewed perspective. So can a few minutes of prayer. God, thank you for easing my fears and frustrations and putting things in perspective.

September 26

For he shall give his angels charge over thee,
to keep thee in all thy ways.

—Psalm 91:11

Thank you for angels! It is incredible that you so love us, your children, that you sent a heavenly host of angels to guide, protect, and inspire us.

September 27

Above all, taking the shield of faith, wherewith ye shall
be able to quench all the fiery darts of the wicked.

—Ephesians 6:16

What are some "flaming darts" that might come in our direction? Doubt and fear, sadness and depression? Temptations, both to the body and the spirit? What about financial and employment problems, marriage problems, and health problems?

All these and more might be the "flaming darts" spoken of in the Bible. But we must remember we have faith as our shield! A shield is a versatile and effective means of defense in any battle we might face. Our faith, if it is built upon Christ and his teachings, can defend us against any onslaught. Thank you for the shield of faith!

September 28

Speaking of God's faithfulness can be difficult; it might even seem weird to talk about God at times. But we can make talking about God and all that he has done for us a habit that we weave into our daily lives. We can take a step of faith and start speaking about God to someone close to us, even if we feel a bit unsure at first.

An easy way to start is to choose one faithful work that God has done in our lives and confide in one person today. The more of God's faithfulness we begin to share, the more God's faithfulness will be apparent in our world, and the more we will notice it.

September 29

$\mathcal{D}$ear Lord, I am blessed to have such good friends in my life, friends who share my sadness and my joy, my pain and my excitement, and who are always there for me when I need them. Just as I can lean on you for anything, Lord, I know you have given me these angels on earth who I can lean on as well. The love of these wonderful people fills my soul. I could not imagine living without them. May I always do for them what they have done for me.

September 30

God, there are so many times throughout my day when my words don't match my actions. I know others are looking to me to be an example of living rightly, but sometimes I just need help keeping my integrity. Help me to not break promises, to watch what I commit to—or overcommit to—especially if I know in my heart I cannot come through. Most of all, match my outer actions to my inner thoughts so that I am walking the talk.

October 1

*H*ow often do we make plans, only to have them fall apart? When my day doesn't turn out the way I planned, it's easy to become angry. Instead, I look for ways to make the day special in a different way and thank God for showing me a new path. Lord, teach me to have a flexible heart and be willing to spend my time as you see fit, not as I do, and to open my eyes to the beauty of the unexpected.

October 2

And the bow shall be in the cloud; and I will look
upon it, that I may remember the everlasting covenant
between God and every living creature
of all flesh that is upon the earth.

—Genesis 9:16

Thank you, Lord, for the beauty of a rainbow. What a contrast that peaceful, glowing bow is to the tempest of the storm that came before it! Help me see rainbows as your promise to the world that beauty and happiness can come after pain and brighten my world again.

October 3

Where no counsel is, the people fall:
but in the multitude of counsellors there is safety.
—Proverbs 11:14

Who guides and protects me in my life? Today, I am grateful for the people who have brought me to where I am today and who always have my best interests at heart. I may not always have appreciated their guidance, but I know deep down they always meant well. In the same way, Lord, let me accept and appreciate your guidance in my life.

October 4

And whatsoever ye do, do it heartily, as to the Lord,
and not unto men; Knowing that of the Lord
ye shall receive the reward of the inheritance:
for ye serve the Lord Christ.

—Colossians 3:23–24

I look around and see there is work to be done. Thank you for the gift of work to do. Guide my hands that they may help others. Guide my heart to see where there is need and how to respond to it. Guide my thoughts to know that even if I can only do a little, that is enough to make a difference.

October 5

Thank you for the bright colors of autumn! I look
around and see the sun in the sky, the clear moon in the
night, the brilliance of the trees. Thank you, Lord, for
blessing me with color in my life. I know that even the
darkest, dreariest days cannot last forever, just as the
memory of storms fades during a glorious sunny day.

October 6

The noise of my children fills my heart. I rejoice in their laughter and loud voices. Some days I may not appreciate the tumult children bring into my life. Help me to appreciate their moods, even when they are not always bright and happy. Lead me to be grateful for how much fun childhood can be. Thank you for letting me join my children in enjoying this special time.

October 7

I do not take enough time to appreciate my heritage. Thank you, God, for giving me this gift. Let me take time to recall special traditions from my homeland and remember to pass them on to my children. I am grateful for the heritage that makes me special yet links me to countless other people, past, present, and future.

October 8

But thou, when thou prayest, enter into thy closet,
and when thou hast shut thy door,
pray to thy Father which is in secret;
and thy Father which seeth in secret
shall reward thee openly.

—Matthew 6:6

Today I feel alone, yet I am not lonely. There is peace in solitude and rejuvenation in the quiet of being alone. Lead my thoughts to restful healing, Lord. Help me use this time alone to find myself and reach deep inside my heart and mind to find peace. I rejoice in being away from the noise and clatter of everyday life and praise God for letting me have this time for myself.

October 9

Sing unto him a new song;
play skilfully with a loud noise.

—Psalm 33:3

Music fills my heart today! I am so grateful for music in all its forms: the loud thump of rock music, the pretty complexities of a classical symphony, the simple melody of a whistled tune. Thank you, God, for putting music into the world and letting it fill my heart with emotion.

October 10

And after the earthquake a fire;
but the Lord was not in the fire:
and after the fire a still small voice.

—1 Kings 19:12

*L*ord, help me
hear that "still
small voice"
in the world.
So often I am
surrounded
by the noise of
others and the
noise I make

myself. Thank you for reminding me to listen to the
small sounds and see your glory in little things. Help
me listen and hear you in the whispers of the world.

October 11

I will speak of the glorious honour of thy majesty,
and of thy wondrous works.

—Psalm 145:5

Today I take joy in nature. I look around and see all that you have made. The natural world is full of your presence. Thank you for the birds migrating overhead, for the wind's breath, even for the violence of a thunderstorm. I know that everything came to be by your hand, and the world around me is a blessing in my life.

October 12

Thank you for the difficult people in my life. They show me that not everything can be easy. When I try to connect with someone who is hard to get along with or who doesn't agree with me, I think of how Jesus reached out even to those who did not agree with him. Allow me to be like Jesus and be thankful for the opportunity to extend my heart to everyone.

October 13

That I will give you the rain of your land
in his due season, the first rain and the latter rain,
that thou mayest gather in thy corn,
and thy wine, and thine oil.

—Deuteronomy 11:14

Rain patters down, making puddles everywhere. I wasn't
expecting the rain, but I am grateful for its beauty. I look
up and see the thickness of the gray clouds and think of
a soft blanket. I
listen to the rain
pour down and
think of how it
waters the earth
to bring new
life. Thank you,
Lord, for the gift
of a rainy day.

October 14

Thank you for my community. As I run my errands and conduct my business, let me remember to be grateful for everyone who helps me. From a clerk at the store to the police officer keeping me safe, my community is filled with people who help others. Thank you, Lord, for putting these people in my life and for giving me the chance to know them. May I always work to make my community a better place.

October 15

A kind act by a stranger is a wonderful surprise! I don't expect someone to let me go ahead in line at the store or to return an item I had lost. What a blessing it is when people reach out to others. Thank you for the small acts that make my day better, and thank you for the opportunity to be a blessing to others by finding small ways to make their day brighter.

October 16

When I don't feel well, it is easy to feel sorry for myself. Then I remember the people who support me and help me when I am unwell. Thank you for the friends and family, the neighbors and coworkers, the nurses and doctors, and everyone else who goes out of the way to brighten my day and make me see a ray of light in the darkness.

October 17

*And it came to pass, that, as he was praying
in a certain place, when he ceased, one of his disciples
said unto him, Lord, teach us to pray.*

—Luke 11: 1

*L*ord, thank you for the gift of prayer. What an amazing gift it is to be able to speak to you any time I need to. May I remember to not only seek you in times of need, but to thank you for all the blessings in my life. May my time in prayer bring me closer to you and help me be grateful for all the wonderful things in my life.

October 18

I went out recently at a time when the roads were filled with school buses. As I watch children get on the buses that take them to school, I am thankful for my own school days. Thank you, Lord, for my education and the doors it has opened to me. Thank you for the friends I made, the rules I learned, and the teachers who guided me and helped me find my place in the world.

October 19

*W*hat a gift friendship is! I am grateful for my friends. Some friends have known me for many years. We grew up together and watched each other change and grow. Other friends are newer, but no less dear. Thank you, Lord, for all the friends you have placed in my life and for the memories we have created together.

October 20

*For I reckon that the sufferings of this present time
are not worthy to be compared with the glory
which shall be revealed in us.*

—Romans 8:18

*I*t's hard to be grateful for difficult times. Help me to see my trials as an opportunity to grow and change. Help me reach out to others who are suffering their own difficult times. Thank you, God, for the chance to know you better through my suffering. Help me remember and be grateful for the suffering you endured to help me. Let me find the bright side of every trial and the strength to be grateful for the test.

October 21

No man, when he hath lighted a candle,
putteth it in a secret place, neither under a bushel,
but on a candlestick that they which come in
may see the light.

—Luke 11:33

Thank you, Lord, for the inner light that shines within me. Help me to show that light to others and not hide it deep inside myself. Thank you for my talents and the things that I am good at. May I never forget how grateful I am to be able to share my abilities and bring joy to others.

October 22

To every thing there is a season, and a time to every purpose under the heaven.

—Ecclesiastes 3:1

Look at the clock. What time is it? Is it time to go? Are we running out of time? I need more time! Lord, help me to stop and relax and enjoy time instead of feeling like it is my enemy. Help me be grateful for each minute and the special joys it brings. Sometimes I need to slow down and think of time as my friend. Thank you, Lord, for time and the gifts it brings me.

October 23

Today I am thankful for my family. My parents, my siblings, my cousins and aunts and uncles…all are part of my family and my life. I may not be close to everyone or see everyone as often as I'd like, but I am grateful for their presence in my life. My family is a big part of who I am today. I need to thank them for that gift, even as I thank God for putting these special people in my life.

October 24

$\mathcal{E}$very day is a journey through time and space. Thank you, Lord, for the journeys that make up my life and take me to amazing places. I am grateful for the things I've learned on my life's journey. Allow me to appreciate the journey more than the destination and keep an open mind for the unexpected gifts on the road. I may not always end up where I thought I would, but I am grateful for the paths I travel!

October 25

What a wonderful gift a book is! Thank you, Lord, for the gift of books, for words and poetry and stories. When I pick up a good book, I am taken away to another place and have the chance to meet amazing people. Thank you for the writers who create the books I love and who have invited me into their worlds.

October 26

O give thanks unto the Lord; for he is good:
because his mercy endureth for ever.

—Psalm 118:1

I am thankful to the
Lord for His gift of
forgiveness. I know I am
not perfect and I know I
make mistakes. Grant me
the wisdom and grace to
know when I am wrong
and to ask for forgiveness.
Give me a sense of
gratitude toward those
who forgive my errors,
and help me forgive others
who have offended me.

October 27

$\mathscr{I}$ am grateful for differences. How boring it would be if every person was the same! How thankful I am not to live in a world full of clones. It's easy to judge others who are different from me, but it is those differences that make the world a wonderful, exciting, and interesting place! Thank you, Lord, for making each person unique and help me to be proud of my own uniqueness.

October 28

Every moving thing that liveth shall be meat for you;
even as the green herb have I given you all things.

—Genesis 9:3

When I go to the supermarket, I am amazed at all the food I find there! As I walk down the store aisles, gratitude fills me for everyone who makes food available to me. I give thanks to the farmers and manufacturers, to those who grow the food and those who package and transport it to me. May I always appreciate their hard work and the bounty they produce.

October 29

$\mathcal{T}$oday my mind is thinking of places far away from me. I am grateful for the places I have traveled to and the opportunity to see new things and meet new people. I am grateful for the places I haven't seen and the anticipation and promise of trips to come. Thank you, Lord, for making it possible for me to leave my surroundings and visit new places.

October 30

Thank you, God, for second chances. Sometimes I feel like I can't do anything right. It's embarrassing to make mistakes. It's embarrassing to show others that I am less than perfect. Thank you for giving me the chance to try again, to make things right, and to improve myself. Help me find the courage to try again and show the world my best qualities!

October 31

*H*appy Halloween! Even though Halloween is built around fear, it can also be a time of joy and gratitude. Thank you for the joy I feel when I see children dressed in costume and enjoying their special night. Thank you for a day when everyone can be as weird as they want to be. Thank you for letting us celebrate the unusual and see the world in a different way.

November 1

*L*ord, sometimes I get frustrated, especially when I have to face something new. Thank you for giving me an open heart. Help me accept change and rejoice in new experiences and new people. Help me to be grateful for new opportunities and always see the good things even when I am afraid to try something new.

November 2

Which now of these three, thinkest thou,
was neighbour unto him that fell among the thieves?
And he said, He that shewed mercy on him.
Then said Jesus unto him, Go, and do thou likewise.

—Luke 10:36–37

A good neighbor is a blessing! I am so grateful for the neighbors I have known and who have become my friends just by virtue of living close by. Together we have faced problems and shared memories. Thank you, Lord, for giving me good neighbors who will stand beside me and help make all our lives more complete.

November 3

*And let the beauty of the Lord our God be upon us:
and establish thou the work of our hands upon us; yea,
the work of our hands establish thou it.*

—Psalm 90:17

God, help me notice the little things and be grateful for them. All too often, we rush through life and don't notice the blessings all around us. I am grateful for the chance to see beauty in the smallest details. Help me remember to slow down and look. I am grateful for the little bits of beauty scattered through my day.

November 4

For the kingdom is the Lord's:
and he is the governor among the nations.

—Psalm 22:28

Thank you for our leaders. I might not always agree with them, but it is good to have people who will take charge and lead us. Help me remember to be thankful for those who dedicate their lives to public service, and help me to appreciate their vision of a brighter future.

November 5

Lord, I see you in the beauty of the autumn. Thank
you for the brilliant colors of the trees. Thank you
for the crisp, cool air that refreshes me. I am blessed
to see autumn's beauty everywhere I go. Thank you
for showing me that a time of change can be one of
the most gorgeous seasons on Earth.

November 6

*I*t's amazing how much joy an animal can bring into our lives. Today I am thankful for my pets—the ones I've had and the ones I know now. I am grateful for their love and companionship, and for somehow knowing when I need a hug or a cuddle. Sometimes it is good to just talk to animals and feel like they are really listening. Thank you, Lord, for the gift of animal companions.

November 7

Too often we hop in our cars or take the bus or train without thinking about how much these ways of transportation make our lives easier. I am grateful for transportation that helps me reach my destinations more quickly. How wonderful it is to get somewhere in just a few minutes or be able to visit someone who lives far away! With every bump of the wheels, may I be grateful for the machines that take me where I need to go.

November 8

As every man hath received the gift,
even so minister the same one to another,
as good stewards of the manifold grace of God.

—1 Peter 4:10

Thank you, Lord, for teachers. How can I ever repay the men and women who taught me and opened my eyes to the world? How can I ever truly thank the people who teach my children and guide them on their journey through life? I am so grateful for those who teach and mentor. Thank you for giving us knowledge and wisdom to carry on life's path.

November 9

All the days of the afflicted are evil,
but he that is of a merry heart
hath a continual feast.

—Proverbs 15:15

Today I am going to treat myself! Thank you for the opportunity to do something special "just because." Thank you for giving me the chance to reward myself just for being me. I am grateful for these little joys and for the ability to recognize that I am worthy of pampering. My life is special, and today I am thankful for the chance to rejoice in myself.

November 10

If ye abide in me, and my words abide in you,
ye shall ask what ye will, and it shall be done unto you.

—John 15:7

How good it is to talk to God! Formal prayer is important, but today I just want to pour out my heart and speak to God in my own words. Thank you for the opportunity to talk to you as a friend. Thank you for listening to my prayers and understanding my heart.

November 11

Have not I commanded thee? Be strong and
of a good courage; be not afraid,
neither be thou dismayed: for the Lord
thy God is with thee whithersoever thou goest.

—Joshua 1:9

Thank you for our
veterans and those who
serve in the military. May
I always remember those
who have given up their
day-to-day lives just to
keep me and my country
safe and secure. Help
me to show my gratitude
toward the veterans I meet
and always remember to
honor their sacrifices.

November 12

How different our lives would be without inventions! When I think back to what life must have been like one hundred years ago, I am grateful for the things that make my life easier. I am glad to have machines to help me cook, clean, and stay entertained. Thank you, God, for inspiring those who came up the inventions that make my life so much easier than my ancestors' lives.

November 13

Thank you for the gift of writing. What a joy it is to express myself through words! A letter, a diary entry, a blog, or a report...all these things are ways I can share my thoughts and knowledge with the world. I am grateful for the chance to express myself and pray that God will guide my pen every time I write.

November 14

Now also when I am old and greyheaded, O God,
forsake me not; until I have shewed thy strength unto this
generation, and thy power to every one that is to come.

—Psalm 71:18

Where would we be without our elders? When I
think about the people who came before me, I am
filled with gratitude for their hard work and sacrifices.

It is good to remember
what they did and how they
lived. Thank you, Lord, for
giving us strong forebears
who shaped the world and
always looked toward creating
a better future. Without
them, my life would be very
different. Help me appreciate
and value the past.

November 15

And so he that had received five talents came and
brought other five talents, saying, Lord,
thou deliveredst unto me five talents: behold,
I have gained beside them five talents more.
His lord said unto him, Well done, thou good and
faithful servant: thou hast been faithful
over a few things, I will make thee ruler
over many things: enter thou into the joy of thy lord.
—Matthew 25:20–21

Today I will find a way to share
my gifts with others. It might be
something small, but I want to find
a way to give something of myself.
Thank you, Lord, for being able to
share our gifts and for being givers.
Even a small gift is a blessing, and I
am grateful to both give and receive.

November 16

How excited I am when I get a new phone or a new computer! It may be frustrating to learn new techniques, but I am grateful for how they improve my life. Technology helps me stay in touch with people who are far away and share news in an instant. I am grateful for the way technology has made the world a smaller place and how it helps keeps people together.

November 17

Today I am thankful for the gift of laughter. How wonderful it is to let out a big belly laugh and feel joy rush through my entire body! Thank you for the people who make me laugh, whether it is a neighbor or friend or a performer on television. Thank you for allowing me to experience joy bursting out of me, and help me make others feel happy with my laughter as well.

November 18

*The stone which the builders refused is become
the head stone of the corner. This is the Lord's doing;
it is marvellous in our eyes.*

—Psalm 118:22–23

How wonderful when God shows us the beauty in something we thought was worthless! I am grateful for the times God opened my eyes to unexpected

beauty. Help me to keep my mind open to the wonders all around me and to appreciate everything I see, no matter how insignificant it may seem.

November 19

Thank you, Lord, for the hobbies that I enjoy. How much joy I get out of these pleasures! Thank you for the chance to create, play, and enjoy. I am grateful for the people who share my hobby and who have become my friends. What a gift to share the joy of our pastimes together!

November 20

*But they that wait upon the Lord shall renew
their strength; they shall mount up with wings as eagles;
they shall run, and not be weary;
and they shall walk, and not faint.*

—Isaiah 40:31

It is hard to be patient, but I am grateful for that gift.
Whether it is waiting in line or anticipating a coming
event, patience is a wonderful way to slow down and
appreciate what is coming. Thank you for the gift of
patience and the ability
to take my time and savor
every moment. Instead of
saying, "I can't wait!" I am
happy to say, "I will wait
my turn" as I anticipate
what is to come.

November 21

*I will praise thee; for I am fearfully
and wonderfully made: marvellous are thy works;
and that my soul knoweth right well.*

—Psalm 139:14

Thank you, God, for my five senses. I am grateful for being able to see, hear, taste, touch, and smell. How wonderful to see nature's beauty, to hear the voices of my loved ones, to taste good food, to smell the fresh scent of spring, and to touch a loved one's skin. My senses let me experience the world, and I give thanks for that gift today.

November 22

While the earth remaineth, seedtime and harvest,
and cold and heat, and summer and winter,
and day and night shall not cease.

—Genesis 8:22

Thank you, Lord, at the harvest time. Thank you for the plants that grow to give us food and thank you for the people who grow them. The Earth's bounty is a miracle! As I enjoy fresh food, may I always be grateful for what I eat and the nutrition it provides.

November 23

Taking part in family traditions is such a joyous experience! Today I will take time to recall the traditions I experienced as a child and the family times I shared with those around me. I am grateful for those memories and for the opportunity to share those traditions with my family and friends today. Continuing a tradition feels like taking joyful steps along a path from the past to the future.

November 24

Come, ye thankful people, come,

Raise the song of harvest home!

All is safely gathered in,

Ere the winter storms begin;

God, our Maker, doth provide

For our wants to be supplied;

Come to God's own temple, come;

Raise the song of harvest home!

Henry Alford, "Come, Ye Thankful People Come"

November 25

Through wisdom is an house builded;
and by understanding it is established.

—Proverbs 24:3

I am so grateful for my home! It may not be fancy, but it is my own place. How lucky I am to have a place to live safely. How good it is sometimes to retreat from the world and be alone with my things, my routines, and my space. Thank you, Lord, for giving me shelter and a place to call my own.

November 26

Verily, verily, I say unto you, He that believeth on me,
the works that I do shall he do also; and greater works
than these shall he do; because I go unto my Father.

—John 14:12

Today I will think about
the miracles in my life.
I am thankful that God
gives me these special
gifts. Miracles remind me
that God is always in my
life. Thank you, Lord,
for showing me your
power and surprising me
with these moments of
grace. Help me see your
hand at work and trust
that your way is the best.

November 27

*The earth is the Lord's, and the fulness thereof;
the world, and they that dwell therein.*

—Psalm 24:1

*H*ow beautiful is the work of your hands, Lord! I am grateful for the world of nature. How wonderful it is to see the plants and animals you have created. How

awesome is your power on the shape of the Earth! Thank you, Lord, for making the landscape and creating so much beauty in the natural world.

November 28

My son, eat thou honey, because it is good;
and the honeycomb, which is sweet to thy taste.

—Proverbs 24:13

How grateful I am for the sweet things I eat! Of course, I don't want to overindulge, but I get so much enjoyment out of the sweet taste! Thank you, God, for creating sweet foods. Help me enjoy them in moderation and always praise you for the sweetness in my life.

November 29

How glad I am that we have tools to help us work!
Even a tool as simple as a hammer or a screwdriver can
make a job easier. Thank you, Lord, for giving us the
tools we need to do our jobs. Help us to be tools as well
and to make others lives easier through our assistance.

November 30

*Be strong and of a good courage, fear not, nor be afraid
of them: for the Lord thy God, he it is that doth go
with thee; he will not fail thee, nor forsake thee.*
—Deuteronomy 31:6

Sometimes it is so hard to take chances! Thank you, God, for giving me the courage to take a chance and try something new. I am so glad to be able to step out of my comfort zone and find the courage to change. What a gift to know that taking a chance could change my life! Thank you for the excitement of being brave.

December 1

Medicine is such a great gift! I wonder what the wise men and women in olden times would think of the medicines we have today. Thank you, Lord, for giving doctors and scientists the desire and the wisdom to create medicines that help so many people every day. Thank you for their work making my life easier, and for making what was once impossible, very possible today.

December 2

Two are better than one;
because they have a good reward for their labour.

—Ecclesiastes 4:9

$\mathcal{I}$ look around at work and think how wonderful it is that so many different people can become a team. Thank you, Lord, for my coworkers and supervisors. We may have our differences and our dark moments, but it is good to know that we are all working together toward a

common goal. Thank you for the friendships I develop with my coworkers and for bringing us together in a special place.

December 3

He caused an east wind to blow in the heaven:
and by his power he brought in the south wind.

—Psalm 78:26

Listen to the wind! I am thankful for its power. The wind is a gift that freshens the air and scrubs it clean. Without the wind, our weather would never change. Thank you, God, for the blessing of the wind and the power it has to change our world and make all things fresh and new.

December 4

*H*ow exciting it is to see and hear the busy hum of a city! I am thankful for all the people who live and work in cities. They have created places that thrum with life and energy. Great things can come from that energy, and I am grateful for the experiences cities provide to all of us.

December 5

What a joyful noise is the sound of children playing!
Thank you for the chance to play with my children, to be
silly with them, and to enter their world and share their
zest for life. Thank you for allowing me to be young again
as I share their joy and their imagination. Thank you
for the gift of
having a child's
joy. Thank you
for the chance
to share with
them the joy
of singing and
praising you.

December 6

If any of you lack wisdom, let him ask of God,
that giveth to all men liberally, and upbraideth not;
and it shall be given him.

—James 1:5

Thank you for people who share their wisdom. Sometimes I may think I know everything, but it is good to realize that there are many people who are smarter than me. What a gift to receive their guidance in my life! Help me to have a listening ear and always be grateful for those who want to help me.

December 7

The flowers appear on the earth;
the time of the singing of birds is come.

—Song of Solomon 2:12

Today, in the dreary
days as we head toward
winter, I celebrate
flowers. How wonderful
it is to see their bright
colors. I am grateful
for the chance to bring
flowers into my home to
brighten a dreary day.
Thank you for the colors
and smells of spring
and the opportunity to
welcome them into my
life at any time of year.

December 8

*I am the door: by me if any man enter in,
he shall be saved, and shall go in and out,
and find pasture.*

—John 10:9

An open door is an
invitation. Just as the gates
of Heaven are open to all
who follows God's will,
an open door invites me
in to experience new joys
and revelations. Thank
you, God, for allowing me
to see the open doors in
my life and take advantage
of new experiences. Let
me walk through them
with Jesus at my side.

December 9

Praise the Lord from the earth,
ye dragons, and all deeps:

Fire, and hail; snow, and vapours;
stormy wind fulfilling his word:

Mountains, and all hills; fruitful trees, and all cedars.
—Psalm 148:7–9

Thank you, Lord, for the signs of your power. Thank you for the awe I feel during a thunderstorm or at the sight of a monument in nature. Thank you for the thrill I feel when I see one of your works in all its glory. It is good to know your power and feel its presence in my life.

December 10

Yea, though I walk through the valley of the shadow of death,

I will fear no evil: for thou art with me;

thy rod and thy staff they comfort me.

Thou preparest a table before me

in the presence of mine enemies:

thou anointest my head with oil;

my cup runneth over.

Surely goodness and mercy shall follow me

all the days of my life:

and I will dwell in the house of the Lord for ever.

—Psalm 23:4–6

Thank you, mighty God, for your promises.
Thank you for being my shield.

December 11

O Zion, that bringest good tidings,
get thee up into the high mountain; O Jerusalem,
that bringest good tidings, lift up thy voice with strength;
lift it up, be not afraid; say unto the cities of Judah,
Behold your God!

—Isaiah 40:9

Thank you for
Advent, for this
season of preparation
and anticipation.
During all the hustle
and bustle of buying
gifts and putting up
decoration, please help
me to keep Jesus at the
center of my thoughts.

December 12

*And it came to pass, that, when Elisabeth heard
the salutation of Mary, the babe leaped in her womb;
and Elisabeth was filled with the Holy Ghost: And she
spake out with a loud voice, and said, Blessed art thou
among women, and blessed is the fruit of thy womb.*

—Luke 1:41–42

The story of Elisabeth and Zacharias, the parents of
John the Baptist, is a powerful one. Zacharias doubts
the angel's words and is stricken silent; when his son is
born and his voice returns, he praises God immediately.
How can I too turn my moments of doubt into praise?
Elisabeth had the wisdom to interpret the meaning of
the babe leaping in her womb,

and did not stay silent. Let
me be like Elisabeth when I
recognize God's presence in
my life, astounded and joyful.

December 13

In those days came John the Baptist,
preaching in the wilderness of Judaea, And saying,
Repent ye: for the kingdom of heaven is at hand.
—Matthew 3:1–2

John the Baptist, like many of the prophets, isn't a comfortable figure—he's intense and uncompromising, unafraid to name sinful behavior for what it is. It can be easier to jeer at him or dismiss him than listen to him seriously. When the prophetic figures in my own life call me to repentance and sacrifice, let me be comfortable with my discomfort. Thank you for those who respond as wholeheartedly as John the Baptist to your call.

December 14

*And there came a certain poor widow, and she threw
in two mites, which make a farthing. And he called
unto him his disciples, and saith unto them, Verily I say
unto you, That this poor widow hath cast more in,
than all they which have cast into the treasury:
For all they did cast in of their abundance; but she of her
want did cast in all that she had, even all her living.*
—Mark 12:42–44

In this season of giving, thank you for those who give
from their heart. Inspire me to give throughout the
year, not just during the
Christmas season. Help
all of us give not just
when we have "extra"
money, but to give as a
regular duty, as one of
our standard expenses.

December 15

Thanks for the foods and drinks of winter that warm us in cold times: hearty soups and fragrant chili, hot chocolate and spicy cider. Thank you for stews left in the slow cooker all day, so that we're welcomed home by good smells. Thank you for comfort foods that warm us from the inside and spicy cinnamon sticks that add a burst of flavor.

December 16

And be ye kind one to another,
tenderhearted, forgiving one another,
even as God for Christ's sake hath forgiven you.
—Ephesians 4:32

Thank you for those people who go out of their way to be kind. Bless them in their turn, so that they receive kindness tenfold.

December 17

And Joseph also went up from Galilee,
out of the city of Nazareth, into Judaea,
unto the city of David, which is called Bethlehem;
(because he was of the house and lineage of David:)
To be taxed with Mary his espoused wife,
being great with child.

—Luke 2:4–5

The trip to Bethlehem cannot have been easy for Mary.
Today I pray for all those who will be traveling this season,
and especially those who will find it
especially challenging: the elderly,
expectant mothers, those traveling
with small children, the disabled.
Thank you for those who are kind
to travelers—helpful employees
at airports or strangers who give
directions to the lost on the road.

December 18

Sometimes it is difficult to appreciate snowy weather, but I thank God for the gift of snow days. How wonderful it is for everyone to be home, safe and warm. On snow days, life returns to a simpler pace and the demands of schedules and responsibilities fall away. Thank you, Lord, for the beauty of the snow and the time it gives us to relax and share quiet times with our loved ones.

December 19

We get fewer Christmas cards in these days of e-mail
and text messages, but they still arrive. Thank you for
the connections that exist that lead us to send these
messages of warmth and cheer. In some cases we hear
from distant friends, and even if we don't talk to
them as much as we used to, it's good to think of them
fondly and hold them up to you in prayer.

December 20

*And we know that all things work together for good
to them that love God, to them who are the called
according to his purpose.*

—Romans 8:28

$\mathscr{L}$ife is like a jigsaw puzzle. When you look at each individual piece, it makes little sense. But when the pieces are all put in their proper place, the end result is a beautiful image, whole and complete. Thus the individual events of your life may make little sense at the time they occur, but when viewed as part of the "big picture," they make all the sense in the world.

December 21

That was the true Light, which lighteth every man that cometh into the world.

—John 1:9

Jesus, Light of the World, thank you for light in all its forms: the full moon shining on snow, the bright clear days after a snowfall, flashlights during power outages, and Christmas lights casting patterns on the ceiling. Thank you for the people who shed light on a knotty problem and the glimmerings of hope in periods of despair. Thank you for lights that guide us on our journeys and candles that spread beautiful scents throughout the room. Thank you for being our Light, casting away all darkness.

December 22

Lord, sometimes the Advent season can be stressful, even difficult. There are moments of awkwardness when someone gives you a gift and you have nothing for them, or vice versa. There are moments of loneliness amid the bustle. The pains of fractured relationships seem especially sharp at this time of the year.

Please keep my eyes focused on you. Help me not get so invested in the idea of a "perfect holiday" that I neglect my daily time in prayer.

December 23

*For in the days of David and Asaph of old
there were chief of the singers, and songs of praise and
thanksgiving unto God.*

—Nehemiah 12:46

Thank you for all those who sing in choirs, now preparing for Christmas services. May their health be good and their voices strong!

December 24

For unto us a child is born, unto us a son is given:
and the government shall be upon his shoulder:
and his name shall be called Wonderful, Counsellor,
The mighty God, The everlasting Father,
The Prince of Peace.

—Isaiah 9:6

What joy you
give to the world.
What joy you
bring to my life.
Thank you, Lord
of the heavens,
for your presence
here on earth.

December 25

Merry Christmas! Thank you, Lord, for this special day. It is the birthday of your son, Jesus, and a bright and beautiful day for the world. Today I am grateful for rebirth, for celebrations, for sharing traditions with the people I love. Thank you for the gift of joy and new life.

December 26

As with gladness, men of old
Did the guiding star behold
As with joy they hailed its light
Leading onward, beaming bright
So, most glorious Lord, may we
Evermore be led to Thee.

As with joyful steps they sped
To that lowly manger bed
There to bend the knee before
Him Whom Heaven and earth adore;
So may we with willing feet
Ever seek Thy mercy seat.

—William C. Dix, "As with Gladness, Men of Old"

December 27

Therefore I say unto you, Take no thought for your life,
what ye shall eat, or what ye shall drink;
nor yet for your body, what ye shall put on. Is not the life
more than meat, and the body than raiment?

—Matthew 6:25

God, please remind me throughout my day that the moment is all I have in which to live. I can't retrieve or retract anything I've done or said just ten minutes ago. Nor can I be sure of what will happen ten minutes  hence. So I pray, Lord, help me leave the past and the future with you so that I can experience the peace of your love in this important bit of eternity called "now."

December 28

Praise ye the Lord.

Praise ye the Lord from the heavens:

praise him in the heights.

Praise ye him, all his angels:

praise ye him, all his hosts.

Praise ye him, sun and moon:

praise him, all ye stars of light.

Praise him, ye heavens of heavens,

and ye waters that be above the heavens.

Let them praise the name of the Lord:

for he commanded, and they were created.

—Psalm 148:1–5

December 29

God, it's a quiet day. Help me pause to listen to you, to talk to you, to enjoy your company. Chase away my guilt and shame and fear, and draw me close to your heart. Remind me that no matter what my earthly roles may be, in your presence I am your child, and you care for me more than I could ever imagine. Let me lean against your heart now, Father, and hear it beating with love for me. Amen.

December 30

Neither do men put new wine into old bottles:
else the bottles break, and the wine runneth out,
and the bottles perish: but they put new wine
into new bottles, and both are preserved.

—Matthew 9:17

As the New Year approaches, please give me the wisdom to know what I need to carry forward into the next year and what I should leave behind. Thank you for this time of reflection. Thank you for this time of renewal and new life. And thank you because, even when New Year's Day has passed on the calendar, you always let me make a fresh start.

December 31

O give thanks unto the God of gods:
for his mercy endureth for ever.

—Psalm 136:2

Thank you, God, for my life. Today I realize I have so much to be thankful for. My life may not be perfect, but nevertheless it is full of good things, of beauty, and of
many wonders. Thank you, Lord, for everything you have given me and the opportunities I've had. Please make me aware of all I have to celebrate and be thankful for.